How to Win

The Sports Competitor's Guide to Success

by

Stephen Walker

ISBN-10: 1478189320
ISBN-13: 978-1478189329

DEDICATION

This book is not dedicated to any of my relatives or people whom I have coached during my lifetime in sport nor to anybody who helped me write it or publish it. No, it is dedicated to all of the athletes whom I have been **unable** to coach. All of those struggling sportsmen and women, young and old , whom I am unable to reach in person and for whom I have written this book. In other words it is dedicated to you. And it is your dedication that will bring about your success. Your dedication to training and your dedication in following the guidelines that I am giving you here in this book that will bring you the rewards you seek. I hope to hear of your success someday.

CONTENTS

PREFACE

I have participated in sports of one kind or another since I was eleven. I have been a life long competitor and I have been involved in encouraging others along the same route to success for almost as long, in the roles of captains of sports teams and as a coach and sometimes just as an enthusiast.

My interest in sport led me to undertake a physical education course upon graduating from University and at the same time I took my first steps towards formal coaching qualifications. I found the topic of sports science so fascinating that I undertook a great deal of reading on its various aspects and this has undoubtedly helped me in my own competition as well as in my coaching of others.

Recently I have found, when in conversation with competitors from sports outside my own personal experience, that I understand, far better than most of them, the underlying foundations of their sports, be they biomechanical, physiological or psychological. I have been able to make helpful suggestions about training, conditioning and preparation for competition simply as a result of being able to ask a few intelligent questions about their sports.

This has led me to the conclusion that unless I put the greater part of my knowledge down on paper, in such a way that an ordinary sportsman or woman can understand it, then only a few people with whom I come into contact will benefit from my experience. Hence this work.

Before you read on, permit me to wish you good luck in your chosen sport, for there is an element of luck in everything; the luck of the draw, accidental good or bad fortune. But if you follow the guidelines ahead and you persist with your sport you will have your share of good luck. I do not doubt that you will be successful because if you were the sort of person to give up after early disappointment then you would not be reading this. You are going to make your own luck!

ACKNOWLEDGMENTS

Mr Jonny Lochner who took charge of my school swimming teams. Karl Gee my coach at Wallasey Athletic Club. My friends, Lawrence Williams and Angus McIntosh, who taught me to row at Bangor. The Dr Dillip Das Gupta, my tutor who fought for me to gain entry into Madeley College of Physical Education. Gordon Richards who inspired me at the Outward Bound School in Aberdovey. Neil Thomas who taught me to scull, who gave me my first novice crew to coach after my Bronze Coaching Award and who put me forward as a founder member of the North West Rowing Coaching Commission. Keith Ovenden and Lt. Cdr. Chris Esplin-Jones who forced me to utilise my Silver Award to coach rowing in the Royal Navy. Mike Fox who was master in charge of rowing at the Kings School, Chester and who encouraged me to take the Gold Award. Dr David Brodie who encouraged me to study for a masters in physiology and who found financial support for the dedicated rowers I was then coaching at Liverpool University. All the coaches who have given presentations at British Rowing seminars over the years from whom I have learned lots. Manchester University for four happy years coaching a rapidly expanding club. Alanda Lennox for her proof reading and encouragement. All my friends at Grosvenor Rowing Club with whom I row and from whom I learn so much each time I teach them something new.

1 BEFORE YOU ENTER THE WOODS
IT'S BETTER TO HAVE A MAP!

1.1 The Road to Success in Sport

To achieve success in any sport you will probably follow a pattern something like this.

First of all you have to choose the right sport if you want to have any chance of winning at it. We all have natural talents and characteristics with which we are born and it should be possible to find a sport at which you can excel, there being so many to choose from these days.

Once you have chosen your sport (or it has chosen you) there will inevitably be skills to be learned so that you can play it or perform within it. Before you can undertake any serious training you need to condition your body so that it can cope with the training. Conditioning usually runs alongside skill acquisition.

After the basic skills have been learned you will need to be coached so as to improve your technique. Proficiency leads to efficiency. Much of the coaching will involve going back to the basic skills that you originally learned because it is too easy for skills to deteriorate under the stress of competition. Competition at a novice level will almost certainly be introduced at this stage.

Having reached a reasonable level of competence in your sport the only way forward into the big league will be by training, both physical, which comes first, and psychological, which comes later.

Finally, for that important championship, you will need fine-tuning to a physical and mental peak.

The process can take weeks, months or years. It can even last decades in some cases. It largely depends upon the level of competition at which you are aiming, see figs 1.1 and 1.2.

The Road to Success in Sport

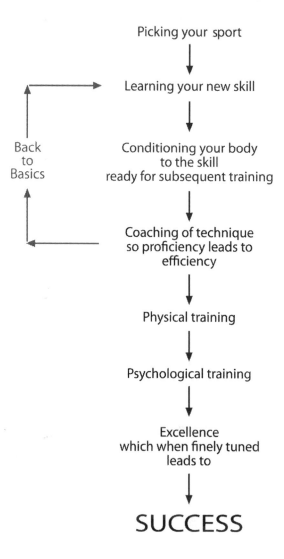

Figure 1.1

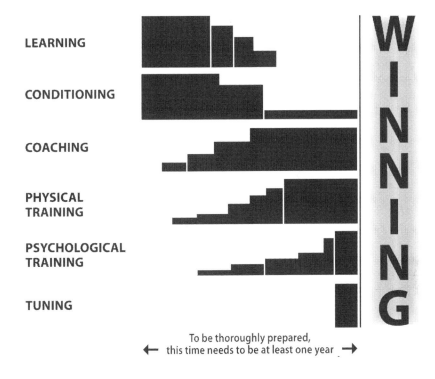

LEARNING

CONDITIONING

COACHING

PHYSICAL
TRAINING

PSYCHOLOGICAL
TRAINING

TUNING

To be thoroughly prepared,
← this time needs to be at least one year →

Figure 1.2

I have included chapters on all these topics and, where necessary, I have expanded them to cover several chapters. This has mainly been necessary to cover the complex and most rewarding subject of physical training, which varies significantly according to what sport you decide on.

Some of the subject matter may seem rather technical. Don't worry about this. **If you find it hard going, skip over it** and look for the **conclusions** or the summaries that I have endeavoured to include along the way.

1.2 Setting out your Goals

Before you read any of the other chapters in this book, which will equip you with lots of important knowledge to help you achieve your aims, you must first decide what those aims are. You must have clarity of purpose.

Here's what to do.

1. Write down your ideal ultimate scenario. Be bold. Be ambitious. Don't cut any corners. Be idealistic, no matter how far fetched it sounds. Forget how long it might take to achieve it. You can plan that later. First you have to know where you are going. What is your wildest dream? Describe it on paper. Do it NOW. Do not read any further until you have taken some time to do this.

2. The next step is to make a **long** list of your desires. I want this. I want that. Don't be ashamed to write down outrageous things. Do not show your list to anybody! You do not want to be inhibited by what other people might say about your ambitions. You must not let other people hold you back. You have to turn the dreams you have written about above into a list that starts with the words: I want. You have to make decisions about what you *really* want. What do you *really* want to do? I mean *really* want. For example you may say:

a. "I want to trash that smug guy, Henry, who beats me every time we compete".

Or you may say:

b. "I to want beat everybody in my county or everyone in the whole country or even everyone in the world". Other people do, so why not you?

Or you may say:

c. "I want our men's and women's clubs to become one club that works as a unit together for the good of the sport". Yes you can want that sort of thing. It's entirely up to you.

Some of the things you want may preclude other things that you want and you have to decide what you *really* want.

I repeat, do not tell anybody about your list in case they knock it. Not even your spouse. You need to be free to think of the wildest, most outrageous things, bounded only my your imagination. If you have somebody looking over your shoulder scoffing at your ambition you might be tempted to edit things out and then you will ultimately underachieve.

You cannot, at this stage make a list for what other people in your team or club may want. That can only be done in a group goal-setting session. First you have to decide what *you* want. And don't even think about what you can or cannot afford. You are inhibiting yourself before you have started if you do that. Just work out what you really want and then you can work out how to achieve it. What you need is images of medals dangling in front of you and outrageously exciting trips abroad. That is the sort of thing I call good stuff. You listen to all the top athletes when they achieve their dreams and you will hear that they have been dreaming about these things for years and years. It did not just happen. Their thoughts became reality.

There are probably some things that you have left out. You can use this methodology to change anything in your life. It is probably frivolous to want to be taller. But if you *really*, *really* wanted to be taller you would find a way. There are ways of increasing bone length, for example, by fracturing them first and then stretching them in a controlled way whilst they are repairing themselves. So if being taller were what you really wanted then you would find a way by using this method, under the correct medical supervision, of course. What I mean is that you might mention that what you want out of all this is to be happy. Or what you want is to be respected. Or what you want is to have fun. You may crave the satisfaction of beating other competitors hollow. But in my experience it is more satisfying to win by a very small margin, especially if you have come through from behind to win. Perhaps this is what you want. Some sports are odd insofar as you can win and still be disgruntled because you know you performed badly. Or you can lose and be beside yourself with joy because you know you never performed better and you could not have fought any harder.

So let's put in a few more life goals. Personal goals. You may have personality traits that you wish to correct. Perhaps you need to be more humble or perhaps you need to be a little more arrogant. Perhaps you don't smile enough. Perhaps you have a short fuse and bite people's heads off. Perhaps you think that you are not very popular and want to be liked more. Anything like this that you know about yourself that you REALLY WANT to change can be put on your wish list. These are all hypothetical examples. I am not prejudging you. If you are embarrassed about them, you do not need to tell anybody about them. Keep them on your private list.

Once you have made your long list see if you can edit it to eliminate duplication and to eliminate things that are not *really* goals but, for example, means of achieving those goals. Sometimes you will put the same objective in more than one way. This might be an indication to you of the importance of that objective. So to help you in the next stage you could perhaps put a star by this objective or put the two similar objectives next to each other and bracket them together.

3. When you have written your list out like that you have to prioritise it. There are two ways of prioritising. You can put at the top of the list the things you want to achieve the most. Or you can put at the top of the list the things that you want to achieve first. Try it both ways and this will help you to work out what is the most important thing to you and what are side issues. To test your priorities you need to ask yourself these questions:

- Which is your top priority?
- Why did you pick this one?
- Is that important to you?
- Why?
- What would be the consequences if you failed to achieve this?
- Would that matter to you?
- Why?

When you have prioritised your list take the top dozen or so and work only with them for the time being. You may not have a dozen. That does not matter. You may not wish to discard some of them to make a dozen. More than a dozen is fine. But try to concentrate on a limited number of objectives. If your list has become so large and unwieldy that you do not know where to start in choosing your priorities, leave it aside for a day or two then it will be easier.

4. After you have chosen your top objectives they need to be rewritten in a special form. First of all you must write what you want in a subtly different way. For example "I want to win everything" should be written as "I always win" or "I win everything I enter" or "I am a winner", whichever you please. "I want to be a great athlete" becomes "I am a great athlete". It is important to do this so that when you read the list you are able to visualise yourself in the situation that you want to be in. It also helps with self-confidence and self-assurance, which are very important. If you say, "I wish our new stadium would be built", somehow it seems intangible, doesn't it. It is like a distant, impossible, pie in the sky thing. But if you say, "I train at a new stadium" then straight away you put yourself in the situation where you are visualising it in your subconscious and it seems real. When it is a reality in your head it will happen.

Now, it is important that you rewrite this list yourself to help clarify these things in your own mind. I could rewrite it for you but it would not be as effective.

Now here is a VERY IMPORTANT PART of the instructions on how to phrase your goals. Check your goals list for the occurrence of the words NOT and NO and try to eliminate them. Goals must be stated positively. So you should not write "I do not want to overdo it". You should write, "I keep things in perspective" or "I am in touch with reality" or "I keep a healthy balance between work and play" or whatever it is that you are really trying to achieve. The reason this is important is that the subconscious is not very good at taking account of the word NOT. Perhaps it is because it works on imagery. I don't know.

The same thing applies to coaching technique. Many coaching manuals will go into great detail about fault spotting and fault correction exercises. This leads rowing coaches for example to say things like "Don't sky your blade!" or "Don't lean away from you rigger" or "Don't grip too tightly". The rower then thinks about the blade skying or about leaning away from the rigger or gripping tightly and then tries NOT to do it. Very negative and too late because the image of skying or leaning away or gripping has already been reinforced in the subconscious by the mere act of thinking about it.

Much better for the coach to present a positive image of what he wants by saying "Take your blade down close to the water for the catch", "lean into the rigger or sit in the middle of the boat" and "keep a light, relaxed grip on the handle".

SO CHECK THE WAY YOUR GOALS HAVE BEEN WRITTEN AND REWRITE ANY THAT HAS BEEN WRITTEN IN A NEGATIVE WAY.

5. What next? This is when you start to use the goals you have listed in a positive way. You have already begun by listing them on paper. The mere act of doing this will have set you apart from ordinary sports competitors. Now you must take positive action.

When you go to bed each night and when you get up each morning, I want you to read your list to yourself, out loud preferably. So you go to sleep with these positive images in your mind and when you wake up and prepare for the day ahead, again your mind is filled with these positive images of your "dreams". It sounds silly, doesn't it? But believe me it works. This is the first stage of implanting positive images in your head for your subconscious to work on.

6. Now we are going to get really clever. This you will not believe until probably six months or a year after you read it and try it. Then when you look back at your goals and see what you have achieved you will be amazed.

First you need to set aside some time to think consciously about how you are going to achieve your aims. You will see all sorts of obstacles in your way. Try to solve these problems with your conscious mind first. Clearly map out the problem. Describe it fully. Define it. Then try to list different ways around the problem. It does not matter if they will work or not. It is just a form of brainstorming.

Then when you have run out of ideas, and this is the cleverest part of everything I am going to tell you, you simply stop thinking about it all and forget about it. Yes, FORGET about it all. You see the subconscious brain is far more powerful at solving problems than the conscious brain. Many thousands of times more powerful. So, provided you have defined the problem sufficiently well and put forward a sufficient variety of possible solutions, the subconscious will beaver away at the problem whilst you are not thinking about it and come up with solutions. It works. Believe me. Ever forgotten anybody's name? The harder you try to remember it the harder it seems to be. And then when you are not thinking about anything in particular, out it pops. What is really happening is that your subconscious brain is working on the problem all the time and when it comes up with the name, the name that you knew all along but could not recall, it brings the name to the attention of the conscious brain. QED.

You can even set a time limit on the problem solving. Say to your subconscious "and I want the answer to this problem by tomorrow afternoon at three o'clock" and it will cobble something together for you by then.

7. Is there anything else you can do? Yes there is. You continue reading your list to yourself every evening and morning but in addition you do the following. Pair your list down to the few most important items. Some things that you are wishing for may really all be the same thing so it may be possible to group them together as one item. You may wish to have a few groups of items; one for academic goals, one for personal goals, one for sport related goals, say, if your list is really very long. Anyway, take one shortlist and then pair it down even more so that each line can be represented by one or two keywords, POWER words.

You take some long-winded objective and pair it down to the bare essentials. The act of doing this is important. It is a bit like describing some complicated part of a sports movement in great detail and practising it in all its component parts. Then summarising it with one short phrase that can be given as an instruction. I went to a lot of trouble explaining what I wanted from the catch (beginning of the stroke) with a rowing crew once and eventually called it "effective reach". If the catches deteriorated, all the cox had to call out was, "Effective Reach" and because everybody knew exactly what that meant and they had practised doing it together, it immediately brought about the desired result. BUT saying "Effective Reach" to another crew would NOT have the same effect because they would not know what I meant by "effective reach".

So when you have whittled down your objective to one key power word or phrase then that will have significant meaning for you and will be as effective as saying the whole original sentence. Next, you sit down (don't lie down in case you fall asleep) and relax until you have reduced your state of arousal to a significantly low level. If you could imagine a scale of arousal from 0 to 10 where 0 is unconscious, 1 is deep sleep, 2 is light sleep etc up to 9 is the level of arousal a sprinter would have when the start gun goes off and 10 is the level of arousal you might have when the fire alarm goes off and you discover it is a real fire, then try to get your arousal level down to about 3 or 4. This is the level that a hypnotist would want you to be in. It is the level at which access can readily be made to the subconscious brain. Then quietly repeat your power words to yourself. This routine will boost the power of the subconscious and help you to achieve your aims more quickly and certainly. There are several methods of relaxing to bring your arousal level down. One way is to monitor your pulse rate and to think it down by controlling your breathing.

1.3 DO IT NOW!

Where will all this lead? Well, you will begin to realise what it is that you have to DO to achieve your aims. You will be able to think laterally and come up with solutions that had not occurred to you previously. Correct analysis of the problem is an important first step.

For example, wishing for a sponsor is perhaps jumping the gun. A sponsor may be part of the solution. But there may be another way of achieving what you want. If you say you want a sponsor, what you are really saying is that you want some kind benefactor to come along and pay for all your expensive sports equipment, travelling expenses and so on. In other words you are saying that you want money. If you realise that most sponsors want a return on their investment and that usually means free press coverage, then you will also realise that you have to work for the money that is being given (paid) to you. It may be that there are other ways of getting the money required or it may be that you do not really need the money to achieve your objectives. Try to open your mind to solutions that are not obvious at first.

START NOW because I am sure you will have read this far without writing down a single thing.

And when you have done all this goal-setting you can read the rest of this book to find out how best to achieve your goals, now that you know what they really are, and then you can make the biggest decision of all, the positive decision to pay the price of your ambition. Mark my words, there will be a price to pay. You may have to:

- train more frequently
- alter your diet
- invest in a coach
- buy better equipment
- give up your job
- delay having a family
- move to another location
- etc.

When you are making your decisions remember that it is an ill wind that blows nobody any good. Think positively about your decisions. If you are going to miss friends by moving away, just think about the new friendships you are going to make when you do move away. And remember you still have your old friends. Always look on the bright side.

And remember that everything that was ever achieved by humankind was first of all a thought! Thoughts become reality.

2 GOOD & BAD HABITS

To win in sport you need good technique; a high degree of skill. Many of today's top sports people learned their skills at an early age from interested teachers or parents who knew what they were doing. They never learned to perform the necessary skills incorrectly. This is a very important point, the fact that they learned their skills correctly in the first place, because it is almost impossible to unlearn a skill. For example, one never forgets how to ride a bicycle. This means that technical faults, once learned and perfected, are difficult to eradicate. Underlying faults in technique tend to lurk in the background and will usually resurface under stress. So it is better not to have learned any faults in the first place. The learning of your skill or skills properly is the first step along the road to success in your sport.

2.1 Methods of Learning

There are two fundamental approaches that can be adopted when learning a new skill. The first is to have the skill broken down for you into easily managed mini-tasks and to build it up by connecting the mini-tasks together until the skill is performed. This is learning by progression.

The second is simply to have somebody demonstrate the skill for you and then have a go yourself. This is learning by discovery.

Learning by Progression

This involves splitting down a skill into its components. The more complex the skill or the more inept you are, the more the skill has to be broken down for you. Gradually you piece together your desired movement by trying always to blend one movement in with the next so that the final movement is smooth and flowing and not fragmented and jerky. Then you practise at successively faster speeds. As the speed increases the skill is likely to break down so be careful not to do too many incorrect repetitions of the movement. Always return to the basic building blocks once the skill has broken down and build up the skill again.

The rule with progressions is to progress from the known to the unknown in easily managed stages.

Examples of Progressions

When learning to jump with a horse you would begin by jumping over trotting poles on the ground. Next you would have your horse jump over crossed poles that are low in the middle. The difficulty of the jump would gradually be increased and eventually you would hope to be able to get your horse to jump over a succession of jumps of different types with merely a bounce in between each one. To progress to jumping diagonally over a series of jumps, which is much more difficult, you would need to return first of all to the trotting poles on the ground but this time lying diagonally to the path of the run you intend to make with your horse.

In trampolining you start simply by bouncing straight up and down. Probably the next easiest thing to do is a tuck jump. After this you might learn an astride jump and finally a piked jump. When somersaulting the easiest way is to tuck. You would then progress to a piked somersault and finally a straight body somersault, which is the most difficult.

When learning to row you would probably be put into a wide stable boat and start by paddling with your arms only, not feathering the blade each stroke but leaving it square to the water all the time. The progression would then involve the introduction of a body swing to increase the length of stroke followed by the use of legs and the sliding seat to achieve an even longer stroke. The progression would then be repeated with blade feathering included. A further progression would be to move into a narrower, faster and less stable boat.

The Discovery Method of Learning

Not many people, if asked to do a backward somersault after just one demonstration, could perform the task without any assistance whatsoever. Clearly this is not an ideal skill to be learned in this fashion. However, there are many skills that can be learned with the briefest of instructions. Some people can watch a skill being performed and just go ahead and do it. Some people are so aware of their own bodies that they can translate words, describing a movement, into the movement itself. With other people one can describe the movement in a hundred different ways and still they will not comprehend. Sometimes their awareness is so poor that one has to ask them to exaggerate a movement in order to achieve what is desired. Sometimes one has to say the opposite of what one wants! With such people learning by discovery may be the only answer.

The key to learning by discovery is the use of internal feedback (within your own body). I will tackle this subject in more detail in chapter 4. Figuring it out for yourself is the essence of learning by discovery. The quick learner requires the minimum of assistance to achieve a satisfactory level of execution of the skill. Indeed, assistance is often destructive and maybe regarded more as interference in the natural learning process. If you are getting along fine, practise whilst things are going well and allow time for assimilation of what is basically the correct movement. Use a broad-brush treatment. The finer points can be dealt with later. When you feel progress is slowing down or difficulties are developing ask for help. The worst thing you can do is to struggle on.

The Practical Approach

Of course, in reality, you always use a bit of both methods of learning with the emphasis on one or the other depending on the complexity of the skill being learned, the danger of the skill being acquired, your aptitude and the expense or fragility of the equipment being used. This last point takes account of the cost of learning by your own mistakes in terms of broken equipment!

There is only one hard and fast rule and it is this: PERFECT PRACTICE MAKES PERFECT. If you practise a skill incorrectly you can get very good at doing it wrongly and the fault, once learned and ingrained will be very difficult to eradicate. Once you have learned a skill, properly or improperly it is difficult to forget it and that is what you have to do if you have a fault in technique. You have to forget it and start again, learning the correct technique. So it is better not to acquire the fault in the first place.

2.2 No Place for Pride

Do not be too proud when learning a new skill to ask for help and constructive criticism. If you just mug through, continuing to practise with imperfect technique, then that is precisely what you'll end up with,

IMPERFECT TECHNIQUE. You will set your learning programme back months unnecessarily. So ask for advice sooner rather than later to check that you have corrected your fault before you practise too much.

2.3 Those Euphoric Moments

You will find that during the learning process you will occasionally improve dramatically and everything will seem right. You catch a glimpse of what it is supposed to feel like. These moments are euphoric. You become very excited about them and want to tell everybody. Go ahead. Enjoy them while you can. That is why you do your sport, to enjoy it. When you stop enjoying it you may as well give up and do another sport.

Those Euphoric Moments

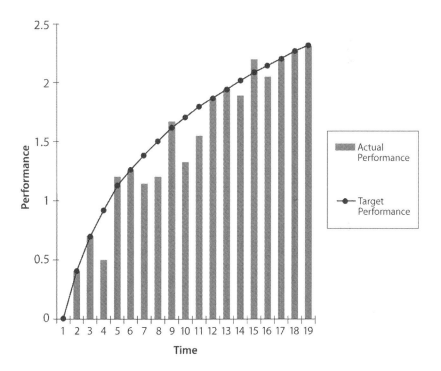

Figure 2.1

Unfortunately, after these great moments, which are often accidental (though it has to be said that the more often you try, the greater the number of opportunities you give yourself to achieve them) you will find, more often than not, that your technique deteriorates. Progress seems to elude you. You hit a plateau or even go backwards. This is quite normal. Those moments of seeming perfection appear lost forever like Sullivan's "Lost Chord", which he discovered one day while seated at the organ.

Do not despair. In fact your technique is probably still at a higher level than it was previously. It just seems lower because you have momentarily achieved a much higher standard. You have now set your sights higher and consequently your less-than-perfect performance disappoints you.

I like to look at this way; if you do not have "down" periods you will not appreciate your "up" periods.

It helps after you have done something well to go back several stages in the learning process to reinforce whatever it was that you learned which led to much improved technique. Build up to it again in the same way and you have a good chance of repeating your golden moment, thereby reinforcing the mental picture of what good technique feels like.

2.4 Too Much Too Soon

Take great care when learning your view skill not to be too daring. Do not bite off more than you can chew. There is an element of danger in most sports and if you give yourself a fright, at almost any stage in your progress towards your ultimate goal you may never reach it.

At the age of 12 in the school gymnasium I tried to do a flick flack (backward handspring or back flip) and landed on my head! It took me till I was 22 before I had another go. This time, with proper supervision and support, I was able to master the move.

"The best way to ruin a young horse is to ask it to do too much too soon". I have heard of numerous examples of this. A horse that would jump fine up to a certain height but never any higher because it had been asked to jump too high when it was a youngster. Another horse that extended itself and really did exceptionally well for its rider going clear over a particularly difficult cross-country fence but which stopped dead each time it subsequently came across a similar looking fence. It had jumped fearlessly over the fence the first time, having trust and confidence in its rider's judgement and its own ability but on the way over it had realised just how big and dangerous this particular fence was. It had survived uninjured this time but it realised that it might not be so lucky next time so it refused to jump.

Taking too big a step in the progression towards your objective is a bigger sin than taking too small a step. In the horse world an animal that has been frightened in this way is called "over-faced". I like the expression because it covers a multitude of situations encountered in other sports for which we have no single expression. The only way to deal with an over-faced animal, be it a horse or a human being, is to go back to basics and build up the necessary skill in small easily digested steps until confidence is restored and fear is inhibited.

The steps must be small enough that the increase in difficulty over the previous step is perceived as being insignificant and the extra daring required is small enough for the perceived level of risk to be affordable. If at any stage during your progression you lose confidence and fumble the skill, go back a few stages and build up your confidence again at a lower risk level, only moving forward again when you are sure of yourself. If you can squeeze another smaller step in between, so much the better.

If you can make careful, measured progress through your sport without ever getting injured or over-faced then you will ultimately perform better. Skiers who have been over-faced, perhaps by a bad accident at high-speed, perhaps not even having an accident but having a sufficiently close shave so as to give themselves a severe fright, are unlikely to perform as well as skiers who have not been over-faced. Fear will make them hold that little bit of speed back and other skiers who do not have that fear may beat them.

2.5 Frequency of Learning Sessions

The psychologists tell us that "a little and often" is best for learning. For example if you have 12 hours available to you than it would be better to learn in twelve one-hour sessions that it would be to learn in four three-hour sessions.

Similarly an hour session, particularly in the very early stages is best split up into 12 five-minute sessions. This is particularly true where an element of fear is involved (however small) such as the fear of falling into water from a canoe, or the fear of falling off a horse, or the fear of drowning when learning to swim. I call this the white-knuckle syndrome. Frightened people tend to freeze, go stiff and grip tight. They panic. In this state they will learn nothing.

If you can learn your skill in a group where initially everybody takes their turn, this will help you enormously.

You will be unlikely to be trying to learn for long enough to get white knuckles.

If you do get white-knuckle syndrome you will shortly be able to relax and recover from your ordeal before you become over-faced.

You will be able to watch other people having a go and this will help you in two further ways.

It will enable you to observe the skill being learned, being practised repeatedly and hopefully being performed reasonably well. This will reinforce for you the mental picture that you need in your head to be able to perform the skill at all, never mind do it well.

It will give you confidence to have another go yourself when you see others having a go.

So when learning, do a LITTLE AND OFTEN and if possible LEARN IN A SMALL GROUP situation. The reason I say small groups is that if you are in too large a group, say more than six, you will not get either sufficient

15

practice or sufficient attention from your teacher for progress to be made at an adequate rate.

2.6 How We Learn

When your brain initiates a movement it has a picture of its own against which to compare the resultant movement and make adjustments during the movement, if it is slow, or make adjustments afterwards, for subsequent repetitions of the movement, if it is fast.

Obviously the quality of the initial picture determines, to a large extent, the final result. The picture can be built up by words from a book or a teacher or by the observation of a film or video or better still by observing a skilled performer in action. The picture can even be built up by touch, as we know that blind and deaf people can learn complex skills. The Worcester School for the blind, for example, has competent rowing crews who compete against sighted rowers!

However, as we know that 90 percent of the information we receive is received through our eyes, then without doubt that initial picture is best established by watching a skilled performer. If an expert provides explanation, drawing your attention to the main points then so much the better. Try to watch from different angles, as a coach would do. Look from the side, from behind, from everywhere. Then try to imagine yourself performing the skill. Consciously reinforce your subconscious image. Shut your eyes and imagine - if you can - what it feels like. Use your other senses now to help build up the total picture. Most movements result in the generation of sounds. Listen to them. Listen to their rhythm. Listen to the sounds the other people make during the same movements. Add them to your internal picture. If a coach can guide your body slowly through the path it will actually take when you perform the skill on your own, this will help to improve the picture. An example of this might be a coach standing next to an oarsman in a rowing tank or on a rowing ergometer and actually guiding the oar handle along the correct path while the oarsman holds onto it. When I was learning to make a horse yield to my leg pressure the trainer grabbed hold of my boot and banged it hard against the horse's side to give me a clear idea of the amount of pressure I should use.

2.7 Feedback

Having established your picture firmly in your mind, using as many senses as possible, you will now have a much better idea of whether or not you are performing your skill correctly when you try it. Around your body is a veritable multitude of sensors called proprioceptors that feed information about the locations of the various body parts back to the brain. It is these proprioceptors which enable you, even with your eyes closed, to touch your left knee with your right heel or your nose with your little finger. I bet you have tried it already. Amazingly accurate, are they not?

The brain is being bombarded continuously with information on your body's whereabouts. It compares this information with the picture of the desired movement and makes compensatory adjustments to the movement in order to reduce any error. If the brain perceives that the movement was good then the picture is reinforced. If the brain perceives that the movement was bad then adjustments are made to the instructions that will be sent out next time from the brain. Then if the subsequent movement is alright the brain reinforces those instructions. This is how we learn.

Of course, if the picture you have built up in your head is incorrect then you might perceive no faults when in fact you have many. This is where the help of external feedback via a video or a coach is essential.

Summary
You learn well by first building as clear a picture as possible in your mind of the skill to be mastered using as many senses as possible. You plant this picture as firmly as possible by trying to imagine yourself performing the movement. Then when you try the movement the brain sends out instructions to the required muscles and compares the actual movement with the picture you have implanted, making any necessary adjustments or corrections so as to reduce the error. If the performance is perceived as good these instructions will be reinforced. If it is perceived as bad they will be adjusted. In order to determine whether your perception of your performance of the skill is correct or not you need EXTERNAL FEEDBACK that will help you either to adjust the picture in your head or to adjust the instructions your brain is sending out to your muscles to perform the skill.

2.8 The role of reflexes

Muscle spindle
Almost everybody has seen the classic knee reflex test and, no doubt, wondered what it is and how it works. Within every muscle group there are special fibres called muscle spindles (because of their shape) with nerve endings on them that act rather like strain gauges. They sense how much the muscles spindle has been stretched and are also sensitive to the speed of stretching.

If the muscles spindle detects a stretch of the muscle over and above what the brain has predetermined there should be in that muscle at that particular time then a strong signal is sent along the nerve fibre from the spindle to the spinal cord. Immediately, another signal is despatched down the motor nerves that control the tension of the muscle surrounding the muscle spindle. This immediate reaction is known as the muscle spindle reflex and you will note that the brain is not involved in the decision to increase tension in the muscle because the reflex mechanism is in the spinal cord. This makes for quicker reaction.

So what is happening when you cross your knees and somebody taps the tendon of the quadriceps muscle group with a rubber hammer? The muscle is stretched, momentarily, beyond where it should be, the muscle spindle reflex comes into operation and the quadriceps tighten up thereby lifting the lower leg.

Now there are hundreds of thousands of reflexes all around the body that enable us to react without thinking and enable us to perform complex skills such and walking without thinking. In most cases the brain can interfere with the reflexes. For example it is possible to think about and control the way that we walk but mostly we do not bother. We can also inhibit reflexes so that in certain circumstances they do not operate. And example of this might be the inhibition of the blink reflex so that a contact lens may be put into the eye or removed from it.

The Golgi Tendon Organ

The Golgi Tendon Organ reflex is one that operates by inhibition. Tendons are portions of strong, white connective tissue that attach the ends of muscles to bones. Between each muscle and tendon is a spindle-like sensor known as the Golgi tendon organ. When the tendon organ is stretched signals are sent along afferent nerves to the spinal cord. There, by inhibitory reflex action, signals are, this time, blocked from the motor nerves to the muscle group in question, thereby preventing any further contraction of the muscle that is attached to the tendon. The muscle then relaxes. This is a safety mechanism designed to prevent injury when too heavy a load is placed on the muscle-tendon combination.

It is by this mechanism that we find a leg may give way underneath us if we accidentally twist an ankle and over stretch a tendon. But we do not encounter the effects of the Golgi Tendon Organ only in situations where there is a danger of over-stressing the muscle tendon-combination. The signals inhibiting the motor neurones are arriving from the Golgi Tendon Organ at the spinal cord all the time and so they provide a form of negative feedback in a complex control system.

Summary

Muscle spindles provide feedback to stimulate a muscle group when there is insufficient tension it that muscle. Golgi Tendon Organs provide feedback to inhibit the stimulus to a muscle group when there is too much tension in the muscle. By acting together in this way a muscle group can be accurately and smoothly controlled. With only one of these reflexes, controlling a muscle would become like driving a car with an engine but no brakes; very difficult to arrive at a precise location at a precise time.

Speed of reflexes

The speed at which reflexes operate is staggering, with reaction times as low as 12 milliseconds. With the involvement of the brain this reaction time may be slowed down to 30 to 40 million seconds. This is still quick but it is only a third of the speed of a reflex.

In order to execute sports skills efficiently, maximum use has to be made of reflexes. Natural reflexes have often to be inhibited and new reflexes established.

Inhibiting Natural Reflexes

When a horse starts to rear, stand on its hind legs, the riders natural reaction is to try to hang on with the legs gripping tightly around the horse's girth.

Figure 2.2

At the same time the inexperienced rider will try to shorten the reins in order to gain more control of the horse. Both these reactions are entirely wrong and will make the horse rear more and possibly even fall over backwards on top of the rider! Gripping tightly with the legs drives the horse's hind quarters forward and pulling on the reins pulls his head backwards. If the horse is already rearing the rider is simply making things worse. This happened to a rider in the Modern Pentathlon at the London 2012 Olympics.

What the rider should do is let the reins loose and keep the legs off the side of the horse so that the horse relaxes and comes down to earth calmly. Needless to say it is not easy to convince yourself when you are on the back of a rearing horse that you should relax. It should be a reflex reaction.

Walking along the slope, neither going up it or down it, the walker's natural reflex is to keep the body weight more over the upper leg than the lower leg, so as not to fall down the hill. The skier, on the other hand, has to learn to inhibit this natural reflex whilst traversing and keep the weight over the lower ski whilst also keeping the upper edge of the ski dug into the snow. The inhibition of natural reflexes in this way is a common occurrence during the acquisition of new sports skills.

Fear is inhibiting

Nowadays in a modern gymnasium you'll find pits full of cubes of foam rubber for gymnasts to land in. The cubes measure about 150 to 225 mm along each side (6-9 inches). The pits are up to 2m deep and to land in one is to land in safety. It appears almost impossible to hurt oneself when falling into a pit of foam cubes. You will find them under the rings, under the horizontal bar, at the end of a floor run, anywhere that they can be of value in providing a safe situation for the gymnasts to learn new moves. I have willingly dared to attempt moves that were beyond my wildest dreams to attempt in the conventional situation. Why? Simply because I had no fear.

Yet if I promptly learned to do a particular move into the pit, I could not do it subsequently without the pit. Not straight away anyway. Why not? Because the fear returned and inhibited me. Fear inhibited my newly learned reflexes and I failed to perform correctly, if at all.

How are you going to get around this sort of problem when it arises? The answer is straightforward. To do a difficult task without any fear and then to do it with maximum fear is too big a step to take. The fear has to be reintroduced gradually. You should perform the task in conditions of gradually increasing danger so that the perceived increase in risk is considered small and affordable given your level of skill at the time.

The principal is exactly the same as I introduced earlier, that is of learning by progression in small manageable steps, going from the known to the unknown, from the familiar to the unfamiliar and in this case from the safe to the dangerous situation.

If you failed to make the progression in small enough steps you run the risk of either becoming over-faced or, worse still, injured or killed!

So if making the steps small enough for you to perceive no substantially increased danger means emptying the pit of cubes, placing a layer of crash mats at the bottom and re-filling the pit with cubes, then that is what you should do.

2.9 Teaching Helps You Learn

I once spent an hour teaching somebody to do a backward somersault from the standing position. I went through all the progressions, covered all the coaching points, supported, provided external feedback and so on. During this time I did not execute one somersault myself but immediately afterwards I did my best ever back somersault. This was a revelation to me. I had done nothing but teach and yet I had learned.

What I had done, of course, was reinforced my own mental picture of the move by talking about it, describing it in detail, explaining it, watching it, feeling it in the supporting I had been doing, listening to it, thinking about it and understanding it.

Every teacher quickly learns that in order to teach a subject one has to understand it far better than one has to understand it to pass an exam on the subject. Students tend to ask awkward questions about unexpected side issues and as a teacher one is expected to give the right answer. This requires a detailed understanding of the subject matter and of related issues.

So if you want to understand your sport, and you need to if you are to perform well yourself, then try teaching beginners as soon as you are able. In passing on your knowledge you will be asked questions, to which you will not know the answers. You in your turn will have to ask somebody else and thereby improve your understanding of your sport. You will be doubly rewarded, as I was in teaching that back somersault, with the gratitude of an enthusiastic pupil and an improvement in your own performance.

2.10 Summary

The practical approach to learning involves a combination of the two approaches, learning by progression and learning by experience. The two main rules to be adhered to are TAKE EASY STEPS in the journey from the known to the unknown and PERFECT PRACTICE MAKES PERFECT. There is no place for pride whilst learning. It is better to ask for advice too soon rather than too late because a fault once learned is very difficult to eradicate.

If you do something right, step back a few stages and repeat the progression up to the correct performance. This way you stand a better chance of doing it right a second time.

Beware of taking too big a step in your progression towards your ultimate goal lest you become over-faced.

Learning in small frequent doses in a small group is usually the ideal situation. Small doses help to alleviate fear, which inhibits learning.

We learn skills by first creating a mental picture of what we are about to do, doing it and then comparing the result with that mental picture. This involves feedback, which can be either internal or external. Both are essential for good progress.

At first the brain is involved in the execution of skills but eventually they are performed largely by reflex. Reflexes can be inhibited and many natural reflexes have to be inhibited for the execution of sports skills.

Fear inhibits reflexes and prevents the proper execution of newly learned skills, so danger has to be introduced progressively.

Teaching will help you learn and understanding will help you perform better.

3 DANGER OF DEATH

This is probably the most important section of this book. Why? Because I believe that the greatest responsibility of all coaches and trainers is the avoidance of injury and illness amongst athletes under their guidance. It is my responsibility, not only to help you to perform well enough to win, but also to see to it that you continue to perform and enjoy your sport.

3.1 *What is Fitness?*

I was perplexed when I was asked this question at P.E. College. I thought I knew then discovered I did not. Is a shot putter likely to be fit enough to run a mile in under four minutes? Unlikely. Would a world-class marathon runner be able to high jump over two metres? Probably not. Could a polo pony survive the Grand National? It would not make it over the first fence. Yet each of these examples cites extremely "fit" individuals in their own field.

In other words fitness is specific to the activity being undertaken. You could be considered "fit" if all you were required to do was sit behind a desk all day. You could be fit to drop or fit for nothing. But to be fit enough to win competition requires training. The training differs from sport to sport and I will look into this in much more detail later but first I want to show you that you need to be fit enough to train. The lower end of the fitness scale I refer to as condition, because fitness could be regarded as a misnomer. Do not be fooled by this remark into believing that if you are already a fit athlete then you do not need to read this chapter. Read on and you will see what I mean.

The Formula 1 racing car might be considered the ultimate machine equivalent to the track runner in athletics. Yet such a car would be no more likely to achieve success in a motor rally than a 10,000m runner would be likely to achieve success in a decathlon. The racing car would slip off a slippery road or go aground on a little bump. The 10,000m runner would strain his shoulder in throwing the javelin or pull a hamstring muscle in the hurdles.

BEFORE YOU CAN GET FIT for an activity you MUST GET INTO CONDITION.

Let me give you a personal example. After a winter of rowing, weight training and trampolining and when I was fit enough to win sculling races, I entered a half-marathon. I had intended to be somewhere else that weekend but owing to a change of plan I found myself with nothing to do so I entered the race at short notice, with NO RUNNING TRAINING. I had had plenty of running experience, however, and I decided that I would like to improve upon my previous half marathon best performance by three minutes.

Well, I achieved my target to within a second. Great! I was well pleased with myself. But I was not well pleased at being nearly crippled after the race. It took me about six weeks before I dared do any training of any sort.

You see my engine was fine but my suspension was not up to the job and by the end of the race my tyres were flat.

If you beef up the engine of a car you must also beef up the brakes, the suspension, even the chassis. Then they can all take the extra loads placed upon them by the beefed up engine and by the extra speed and acceleration to which the car is subjected.

3.2 What Should You Condition?

The same sort of things that when you are conditioned you will subsequently train and a few more besides.

These include:

- joints (and joint capsule)
- bones
- tendons
- ligaments

I mention these first of all because a six-week layoff can cause 30 percent degeneration in the strength of these structures. This is why in the first term back at College after the long summer recess most sports injuries occur during the first few weeks. Over keen but out of condition students playing hard for positions in teams put themselves out of the running simply because of haste.

To give you an idea of the sort of level of conditioning you should achieve before "training" I would suggest that you should be capable of 30 minutes continuous running without strain or consequence the following day. You could replace the word running here with swimming or cycling or sculling or cross-country skiing or aerobics, indeed any activity that can be performed continuously.

To consider harder training you should be capable of running four miles in 30 minutes (three miles for a female).

These are only rules of thumb. Rough guidelines. Clearly if you are already a fit athlete you might easily be able to perform these tasks and yet still be out of condition for an alternative activity. In this case the new activity has to be introduced gradually so that conditioning is achieved. An example might be the introduction of a new exercise into a circuit training routine or into an aerobics session. That one exercise alone can lead to soreness, pain, even injury if it is not introduced properly.

Of course aerobic conditioning is the precursor of aerobic training and likewise strength or speed conditioning should be the precursor of anaerobic training.

3.3 Ventilation

The volume of air you breathe in or out of the lungs in a minute is known as your minute ventilation. This is one of the first things to show an improvement during initial conditioning and will typically improve by 50 percent over four weeks. The improvement is brought about by increases in the rate and the depth of breathing.

Bear in mind that no training effects are permanent and ventilation is no exception. You can lose 50 percent of your lung capacity during a layoff.

Although your maximum minute ventilation will improve with training it is not a limiting factor in the performance of aerobic tasks.

Along with an increase in your maximum minute ventilation will come an improvement in the efficiency with which the gases, oxygen and carbon dioxide, are exchanged in your lungs. All of these improvements will mean that at a given work load your breathing will be less stressful.

To help you introduce the upper chest muscles, which are used in heavy breathing, introduce exercises into your warm up that involve stretching your arms above your head when breathing in. Do not, however, contrive to breathe too heavily for too long without need. This is called hyperventilation and can lead to dizziness, fainting and even death, though this is unusual.

3.4 Muscles

When subjected to aerobic stress the aerobic enzymes will increase in number. These assist in the conversion of fuel to energy and the conversion of spent fuel into usable fuel. Also the number and quality of mitochondria in muscles will increase after only a few weeks. It is in the mitochondria that the aerobic processes take place.

When subjected to anaerobic stress, such as in strength or speed training your muscle fibres will increase in size. Under very severe training, which is not within the scope of this chapter, they may even increase in number within a muscle group. There are other biomechanical changes that take place and also adaptations within the nervous system including changes in the patterns of recruitment of muscle fibres and improvements in synchronisation as outlined in the chapter on learning.

3.5 The Circulation

The number of tiny blood vessels (capillaries) supplying your muscles increases with training so that the blood is able to bring oxygen to the muscles more easily and to take away the waste products, such as lactic acid, more readily.

3.6 Cardiac

Your heart first of all improves its efficiency by filling and emptying more completely. The muscle around the heart improves and finally the volume of your heart increases. These are improvements of major importance.

3.7 Overall

Your body will adapt to the stresses under which it is put. These have to be measured according to your initial fitness but in any NEW activity the stress that you place yourself under should be LOW. Take it easy at first even if it seems ridiculously easy. If you have not done a particular sport, activity, event, exercise or even a simple movement before, or even if you have but it was more than a month ago, and particularly if it was six months since, then break yourself in gently. The temptation to go at something as hard as you used to or as hard as you are used to doing other things can be your downfall.

This is how gardeners injure their backs, often in the first spring weekend's gardening session after a winter of inactivity.

3.8 Hooke's Law

Cast your mind back to early science lessons at School and you may just remember this law, which states that extension is proportional to load applied. You may have done an experiment with a spring and weights to prove its validity.

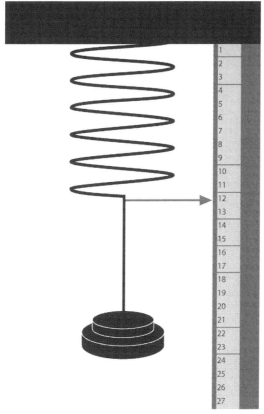

Figure 3.1

The graph below, showing how much the spring extends for a given load, is a straight line, proving that there is a direct relation between the two. The more you pull something the more it stretches. And when you let it go it returns to its original length.

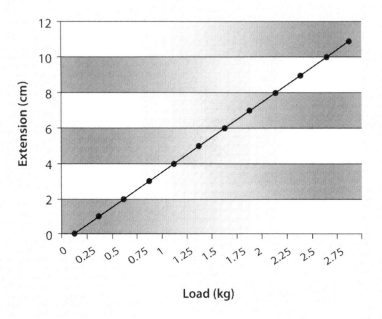

Figure 3.2

Later on in school of course we learn what every inquisitive schoolchild already knew, which is that Hooke's Law is not universally true and only works provided we do not stretch the spring too much! Placing more load on the spring we get a graph like figure 3.3.

Elastic Limit

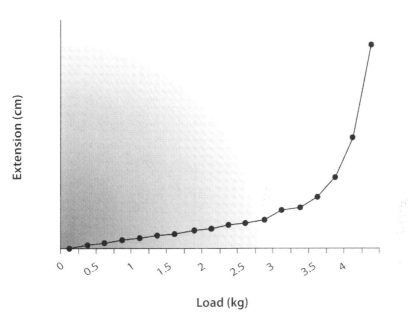

Figure 3.3

Eventually we reach the point where the spring stretches a disproportionately long way for a very small increase in load. This point is known as the elastic limit. Imagine now that you replace the spring with a tendon or ligament. If, somehow, you put too much of a load on a tendon or ligament or a muscle for that matter, eventually you may reach its elastic limit. It will no longer be elastic (which means that it will no longer return to its original length when you remove the load).

Permanent Change in Length

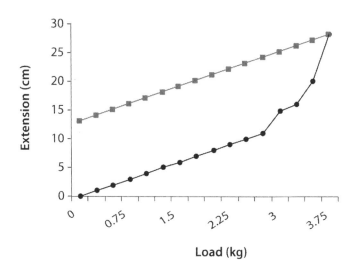

Figure 3.4

This is a catastrophic situation to reach. It means that the tendon or muscle is now too long and this affects the tension that the muscle can subsequently create because it is no longer its "design" length. This assumes that repair is eventually adequate for substantial loads to be applied.

Ligaments (which are used to locate joints) and tendons (which connect muscles to bones) if stretched beyond their elastic limit can no longer perform the job for which they were designed. Supportive bandages can help in some instances but they are never as good as the real things. And how do you bandage a ligament in the spine?

There is only one stage worse that you can reach…

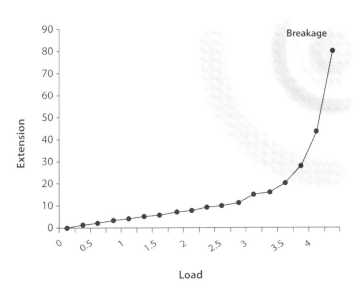

Figure 3.5

Tendons and ligaments are white connective tissue, not made up of living cells and with no blood supply for the nutrients required for growth. REPAIR TAKES MONTHS AND MONTHS!

I hope that the message is coming over loud and clear. Conditioning is essential if you are to enjoy a long, active career in sport.

3.9 Further Tip (The Plasticine Analogy)

Imagine that your ligaments and tendons and muscles are made of Plasticine. When you first get hold of cold Plasticine it is a bit crumbly and prone to break up in your hands. But as you work it in your hands it gets warmer and more pliable, more elastic and its sticks together better so that it can be stretched a long away before it breaks.

Similarly when your ligaments, tendons and muscles are cold they are more vulnerable to strain or tear than when they are warm. So warm up and keep warm, especially in cold weather. Do not do anything vigorous until you are warm and especially DO NOT STRETCH when you are cold. Do not do stretching exercises in the first part of a warm up whilst you are still cold and stiff. Do instead exercises that use up energy and make you sweat. These will get you warm throughout your body. Then when you are warm you can stretch but keep putting in the occasional energetic exercise to prevent you from getting cold.

I learned this lesson the hard way, attending jazz dance classes in which the warm up largely comprised stretching exercises of one sort or another. In dance this is euphemistically known as "technique"! I knew better than to do this, of course, but in a group situation my competitive nature came out and I did not wish to lose face by failing to perform apparently straightforward exercises. Furthermore I used to adhere to the "No Pain, No Gain" philosophy and when my lower back hurt I thought it must be doing me good. The osteopath, whom I consulted later, informed me otherwise. I had strained a ligament in the lumbar region of my spine and this was allowing a disc to slip out of place and press on my spinal cord causing me acute discomfort. Fortunately he was able to put my spine back into place but the ligament, predictably, took ages to repair and of course, because I had stretched it beyond its elastic limit, it has remained vulnerable to injury to this day. You will find that with injuries of this nature. It is commonplace for people to sprain the same ankle over and over again. Once a ligament is over-stretched you are vulnerable. So please, try to avoid injuring them when you can.

If it is cold wear two pairs of socks to keep your ankles warm. Avoid stretching when cold. Get warm and stay warm even if it means wearing stupid looking clothes! Look at the veterans in your sport and see what they wear on cold day. They have learned the hard way too, many of them. Don't let bravado and machismo dictate what you wear. Let other people get injuries then you can have the last laugh.

I remember sitting for two hours before it was my turn to go at the start of a long distance race in winter with snow falling. I was wearing two pairs of socks, a thermal vest and long johns, a club vest and shorts, a T-shirt, tracksuit bottoms, two tracksuit tops, a scarf, a bobble hat and a pair of ski mitts. I looked like a Michelin man but I was still a bit cold. However, I was not as cold as the novice who was up at the start wearing only a white cotton vest and shorts. He was blue with cold! When you get that cold you never get warm. Your muscles do not work properly. You sometimes experience electric shocks down your arms as you straighten them, and you are in grave danger. You could end up suffering from exposure and in a boat you could fall in and drown!

3.10 Post Injury Depression

You may have heard people say that sport is like a drug to them. They have to do it. They are addicted. Indeed they are. The body's own painkiller, a morphine like substance, circulates in the bodies of regularly training sports people. This gives them a feeling of health and well being much as heroine is reputed to do.

And if, because you become injured, you are unable to train you will suffer withdrawal symptoms. I once heard of a runner who became so depressed after injuring himself that he was almost suicidal. What saved him in the end was the suggestion that he should run in a swimming pool. He said it was not as good as real running but it was better than nothing was and it did alleviate his depression.

3.11 Eccentric Muscle Contractions and Muscle Soreness

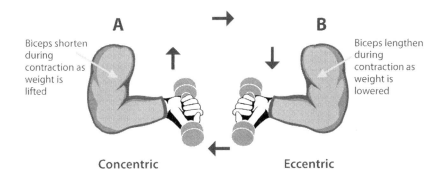

Figure 3.6

If A lifts a heavy weight and passes it to B who then lowers it and passes it back to A and this is repeated a number of times until both A and B are tired then both will probably end up with sore biceps. Of the two, B who has been doing eccentric muscle contractions will have the greater soreness.

Muscle soreness usually appears after about 12 hours and continues, sometimes getting worse for a further 24 hours, sometimes more, sometimes less. Eccentric contractions of muscles are those in which the muscle is lengthening whilst tension is developed it. It is virtually impossible to avoid eccentric contractions when gravity or springs are providing the force against which the muscles are acting. If you lift a weight you will perform concentric muscle contractions, if you do it correctly, but when you put it down again you have to perform eccentric contractions. If you stretch a spring, a chest expander for example, you will use concentric muscle contractions, but if you hold on to it whilst it returns to its original length then you will be doing eccentric contractions. As eccentric muscle contractions lead to great muscle soreness, the East German rowing teams were trained to drop lifted weights in order to avoid the eccentric contractions involved in lowering the weights to the ground again.

A girlfriend of mind once showed interest in the results of some step tests that I had done. They formed part of my assessment of the fitness of members of a University club that I was coaching. She asked if I could give her the step test. So I did. She stepped up and down 30 times a minute for five minutes onto the arm of my sofa, which was about the right height. Two days later she was on the telephone complaining that she could hardly walk and that she had been forced to take a stick to work to help her hobble around! I am afraid I laughed. As she had been stepping up and down leading with her right leg for the whole five-minute test I was able to guess, correctly, that it was her right calf muscle that was sore. You see, every time she landed on the floor she did an eccentric contraction of the right calf muscle. It stretched as she lowered the right heel to the ground, having first touched the ground with her toe, and of course it was bearing her whole weight. The left foot, however, bore no weight as it was already borne by the right foot so she had no soreness in her left calf muscle at all.

It has to be said that people who do step ups regularly as part of their training do not suffer from muscle soreness in either of the calf muscles following a step test. This implies that it is as much the unfamiliarity with the eccentric muscle contractions as the eccentric muscle contractions themselves which lead to delayed muscle soreness.

It is reassuring to know this. If you find yourself stiff and sore in a particular muscle one day it is a relatively easy to think back to what you did the day (or two days) before. You can work out which exercise or new movement you did that might have involved an unfamiliar eccentric muscle contraction of the sore muscle. Armed with this knowledge you can either avoid that exercise again, or reduce the load next time so that you can get in condition for doing it more severely later. You are also that bit more familiar with the pain that goes with muscle soreness. It is important to be able to distinguish between acceptable and unacceptable pain so that you can consult a doctor when you have done yourself some harm.

You can alleviate some of the soreness by stretching and, generally speaking, although stiff and sore you can perform vigorous exercise still and you will not feel so sore whilst you are doing it. The pain will come back though, when you have nothing else to think about.

If you want to discover what harmless delayed muscular soreness feels like and how temporarily crippling it can be then may I recommend horse riding to you if you have never done it. It exercises muscles between the legs that are not normally exercised and the chances are that two days after a two-hour ride you will still be very uncomfortable. But any exercise that you have never done before will lead to muscle soreness. Even sports which are essentially similar in most ways, such as rowing and sculling, tennis and squash, also have essential differences, which, although they may be small, will nevertheless necessitate the use of slightly different muscles and lead to muscle soreness here and there in your body.

There is a danger here in that if you are a fit athlete in one sport, you can actually overdo it in another similar sport for which you are well equipped in almost every respect. Your only shortcoming might be the conditioning of one small muscle. So be careful if you participate in something new, not to play too hard the first few times. Even as simple a thing as sprinting when you are used to long distance running can lead to severe muscle soreness in the back. Yes, the back muscles! It is no accident that sprinters have highly developed musculature in their upper bodies. Sprinting demands it, whereas endurance running does not. The marathon and the 100m although both running events are as different as fencing and water polo in the demands placed upon the body and the training required.

3.12 Machines that Minimise Soreness
The pumping of a bicycle tyre is on example of exercise where concentric muscle contractions take place, without the soreness producing, eccentric muscle contractions taking place. During the recovery phase of each pumping action there is no load. This idea of working against the resistance provided by a hydraulic or pneumatic device has been used in the development of machines for strength training. When you push against one of the levers of such a machine it pushes back at you whilst allowing movement to take place. The speed of the movement does not depend so much on how hard you push as on the setting of the machine. I will discuss these machines in more detail later, but for now it is worth noting that muscular soreness will be less after training on such a machine because during the recovery phase the machine does not resist of its own accord. What I mean by that is that it does not store energy in the same way as a spring or a lifted weight. Consequently you always have to work on it. It never works on you. Thus no muscles are required to work eccentrically and muscle soreness is therefore inhibited.

3.13 Dental Health!
I have used this heading so that you will read it out of curiosity. It is really about total health but dental health forms an important part. An infection in your teeth or gums is every bit as taxing on the body's immune system

resources as an infection anywhere else. A dental check up is included in the prerequisites for selection for many national teams. It is no good getting to the world championships and being below par because of an abscess in your mouth or a virus that settles in your knee (yes this has happened). So take care of your teeth.

More to the point take care of your overall health. It is better to have a week or two or even a month off, whatever is necessary to recover, than it is to be out of action for six months or for ever!

3.14 Recovery from Illness

I will give you an example.

I was coaching a girl who aspired to selection for the Commonwealth games. In September she had an operation on one of her wrists which meant a week off training. This was not so terrible by any means. It was at an unimportant time of the year when the effect of any training done would be immeasurable at the games the following year. But to her it was important time lost and she was keen to get back into training. Then she went down with flu. It was a very severe and worrying attack, which kept her from training for a further week. Really she should have stayed off longer and recuperated completely. But no, time was marching on so back to training she went. A week later she was down with flu again. Another week off. Panic was beginning to set in now. A whole three weeks off training. Calamity! If only she could have been persuaded that it was not that important at that time of the year. Then she went to London for a training weekend and as a result of an accident received a severe blow to her back resulting in badly bruised muscles. We took her to hospital and fortunately nothing was broken but she was in a lot of pain. Two days later she was back training again against my advice! It is very difficult when somebody says that they are all right to argue with him or her. The end of this unfortunate chain of events came during a circuit training session soon afterwards, before she had fully recovered from the back injury, when she pulled an intercostal muscle. Intercostal muscles surround the ribs and are used in heavy breathing. Well, you can imagine that the pain involved with this injury was such that she simply could not do anything at all. It hurt just to breathe.

It took some time to identify exactly what was wrong and various cures and palliatives were tried but after three or four months she was eventually persuaded to change doctor to one who was more in tune with sports people and their injuries. He understood just how important it was to her to get back into training. He gave her an injection into the muscle that had the desired effect within a couple of days and two weeks later she was back in training.

Needless to say she did not make it to the Commonwealth Games. She might have done if each time she had been ill or injured she had not been so hasty to get back into work. Who knows? Some injuries take a very long time to get over and whilst you are recovering you are more susceptible to injuries if you train.

As for training after flu, forget it. Any time that you have a temperature just forget training until you have completely recovered. Otherwise you run the risk of getting myocarditis, inflammation of the heart muscle. Very dangerous. The Swedes lost a succession of top orienteers owing to the athletes continuing training during bouts of flu. Yes, they died!

Often you can cut down the time that you are unable to train by being sensitive to your own condition and stopping training straight away. Once I got into my boat and immediately upon taking my first stroke I realised that something was wrong. I did not at this stage realise it was me. I thought that somebody had altered the gearing of my sculls, thereby making it harder for me to pull the boat through the water. Anyway the boat felt heavier than normal. I did my training session and was five seconds slower on each 250m row than I would have expected to be. This gave me a serious clue. If my gearing had been altered I might have expected to be faster on the first 250m row than on subsequent ones and I would have expected to get progressively slower. But no, I was just consistently slower. In fact, nobody had altered by gearing and the boat was not heavier. I was weaker.

When I got home I went to bed after taking an aspirin and drinking a lot of orange juice. My pulse was abnormally high, around 90 as I remember, so I knew I was ill. With more orange squash and aspirin during the night I simply sweated the fever out and after a day of complete bed rest I felt fine. I was lucky. A quick bout of flu was all it had been. But I was sensible with myself so I was rewarded with a quick recovery.

Following this experience, I was able to spot when the girl who regularly exercised next to me in my aerobics class had a cold before she even knew (by the normal symptoms). I told her that she was not entering into the work with her normal vigour and enthusiasm and wondered if she was ill. She said, "No" but she didn't attend the next two or three classes because of a bad cold. If I can spot this in other people you can spot it in yourself. (This does not mean that you should become a hypochondriac).

On another occasion I was not ill but I did feel very vulnerable and susceptible to injury. I had been doing particularly gruelling one-hour sessions of aerobics three times a week for about eight months when I decided to run in a local 10km road race. I thought that there could hardly have been a muscle in my body that our aerobics instructor could have missed out with the huge variety of exercises that we did. I was wrong. Road running, I discovered, is as different from aerobics as it is from rowing and trampolining. So I got muscle soreness which lasted till the next aerobics session. I felt very vulnerable so I skipped it. It simply was not worth the risk of serious injury. Sore muscles are weak muscles and I was afraid that they would be much more likely to give way in their sore condition. It was better to miss one aerobics class than to be off for several months.

Unfortunately this sort of wisdom tends only to accumulate with age and experience. Learning the hard way. But you do not need to learn the hard way because I am cutting corners for you. I no longer have anything to prove and if you can go out and win without getting injured because you have followed my guidelines then good luck to you.

Remember when you are a top class athlete you are a very finely tuned machine rather like the racing car I mentioned earlier. A spec of dust in the fuel injectors and it comes coughing and spluttering into the pits, firing only on some instead of all its cylinders. When you are at the peak of your form you are much more susceptible to illness or injury. You are so finely tuned that the least little thing will upset you and you will be unable to produce the top class result. Racehorses are just the same. So take extra good care of yourself. Do not abuse your body. Handle it with kid gloves. Wrap it in cotton wool. Do whatever is necessary to keep yourself in good condition for the maximum time.

3.15 Warming Up

Most people include stretching exercises in their warm up routines. Some start with them, without realising that you have to be warm already before you can stretch easily and safely. First you need to warm your soft tissues, those muscles, tendons and ligaments. Then you can strain them by stretching or contracting them but not before.

It does not take much time to get warmed through. Five or ten minutes gentle jogging, with sufficient clothing on, will do the job. The reason for this is simply that in jogging you are using the very large muscle groups in the legs. These produce a lot of power and in the process a lot of waste heat that has to be taken away via the blood to other parts of the body that are cooler. The skin, of course, is the coolest part of the body so when that gets warm you know you have warmed your body through.

After this initial warming you can start to make more exaggerated movements of the limbs more safely. Do not really force anything too hard yet though. Work gently around your body stretching and flexing, twisting and straightening a bit at a time.

Now here is an IMPORTANT POINT. Do not allow your body to get cold. You have warmed it through so that you can stretch and flex safely. If you get cold again you will no longer have the benefit. My advice is to intersperse your stretching exercises with more vigorous exercises such as squat thrusts, squat jumps, burpees or fast running on the spot, which use the leg muscles and thereby pump warm blood around the body.

When you have been around the body once limbering up and keeping warm it is safer for you to do more demanding stretching exercises provided these are going to be of value to you in what follows, either competition or training. But do not overdo it. Particularly do not do stretching or limbering exercises to which you are unaccustomed just before a competition. You will not be conditioned to them and are more liable to injure yourself or make yourself susceptible to an injury during the competition itself.

Your warm up routine before competition should be much the same as before training, not radically different.

Include in your warm up the activity that you are actually going to do. Some rabbits were taken from an area where they were able to run around freely and put in a situation where this was not possible and also they were unable to bear their weight on their legs. X-rays of their knee joints were taken before this period of inactivity, which lasted for an hour, during it, and after it. The results of these x-rays showed that the thickness of the articular cartilage in the knee joints of the rabbits fell by about nine percent after half an hour and a total of approximately 11 percent after the full hour. The articular cartilage is the shiny, smooth, load-bearing surface on the ends of the bones and its thickness clearly affects its shock absorbing properties.

Just imagine yourself now sitting in a car, totally inactive, on the way to an event and imagine what is going to happen to your articular cartilage. Fortunately it was found that when the rabbits were exercised for 10 minutes on a motor driven treadmill cartilage thickness increased so that it was actually about two percent thicker than when the rabbits had just been removed from their spacious hutches. After a further period of inactivity the thickness of the cartilage fell again, much as before.

What this experiment, performed in 1948 by Ingelmark and Ekholm, tells us is that the cartilage responds to exercise, quite quickly. It shows us that the body considers it necessary to have thicker cartilage during exercise than it considers necessary during rest. It shows us that the activity to be undertaken should be included in the warm up so that the appropriate joint cartilage is prepared. And it shows us that there is a particular danger in springing out of bed or out of a car and getting straight on with your training or competition without first of all gently preparing the joints in a warm up.

3.16 Stretching and Flexibility

A word of warning about stretching. You may remember in the section describing the muscle spindle reflex that it is not only responsive to the amount of stretch but also to the speed of stretch. Either way if you bob when stretching, you create a stronger impulse traffic along the nerves coming from the muscle spindles than if you do not bob. Remember that these nerve impulses, when they reach the spinal cord, are immediately translated by reflex action into motor impulses that instruct the muscle group in question to contract. This is not what you want when you are trying to stretch the muscle. You would rather it relaxed a bit.

If you stretch the Golgi Tendon Organ, which you may remember is inserted between the ends of just a few of the muscle fibres in a group and the tendon, then this will send impulses to the spine which will inhibit contraction of the muscle. The question is how do you stretch the Golgi Tendon Organ without at the same time stretching the muscle spindles. The answer is you cannot. The signals from the Golgi Tendon Organ are stronger during a muscle contraction than they are during a muscle stretch for mechanical reasons. This means that they inhibit contraction during a contraction (thereby controlling the contraction) more than they inhibit contraction during a stretch. This makes it difficult to stretch because the muscle spindle reflex creates a strong contraction signal upon stretch and the Golgi Tendon Organ only creates a relatively small relaxation signal during a stretch.

One way to reduce the effects of the muscle spindle reflex and to increase the inhibition of contraction of a muscle, thereby inducing relaxation, is to contract the antagonistic muscle in order to create the stretch. This is a very safe way of stretching. The antagonistic muscle is the muscle that has the opposite action to the muscle in question. Thus the triceps are antagonistic to the biceps because triceps straighten the arm whereas the biceps bend the arm at the elbow.

When you contract your biceps the muscle fibres at either end of the muscle spindle itself are temporarily tensed and this tension stretches the muscle spindle. This creates a signal that reinforces the contraction of the biceps. This signal goes to all the other fibres in the group, not just those in the muscle spindle. At the same time, however, an inhibitory signal is sent to the triceps muscle, which induces relaxation of this muscle. If this were not the case then as soon as the biceps contracted the triceps would be stretched and the triceps muscle spindle reflex would come into operation. The two muscles would therefore always the working hard against one another.

Conclusion

It is safer to stretch your hamstrings by sitting down and doing a slow V sit than it is to bend over from the standing position and bob up and down in order to try to reach the floor with your hands. These principles can be applied to all muscles but if you want some ideas for stretching exercises simply watch a dog or cat when it stretches after waking! Better still, take up yoga. I have.

3.17 Practise Throws

Some Eastern block throwers used to achieve their best results in athletics events with their first throws, having had no practice throws. This has to do with stored energy in the muscles that is available only in that first throw. With the shot, which involves a minimum of eccentric muscle contractions, the risk to athletic tissues is minimal. In all other activities a warm up is safest and the activity itself should be undertaken during the warm up. However, nowadays it is not uncommon for javelin throwers to produce their best throw in their first effort.

3.18 Visual Acuity

Cricket players have found benefit in warming up their eyes before play. This was achieved with a computer driven visual display unit that gave the eyes exercises to do. No doubt there are other sports that might benefit from this sort of warm up.

3.19 The Digestive System Shut Down

One of the main benefits of warm up activity is the splanchnic shunt. This is a change in the flow of blood from the areas of your body concerned with digestion to those concerned with physical activity. The blood vessels carrying blood to the liver, intestines and so on are constricted by visceral (smooth) muscle whereas those supplying the skeletal muscles become dilated. Thus digestion is inhibited and more oxygen carrying blood is available for the muscles. The skin is supplied with blood when necessary to facilitate cooling.

3.20 Winding Down

After vigorous exercise a winding down, warming down or cooling down procedure should be followed. Before the splanchnic shunt reverses the waste products of exercise need to be flushed out of the system otherwise they collect and pool in the muscles where they create stiffness and pain. They also inhibit further performance so if another heat in a competition follows fairly soon afterwards then waste products in the muscles will have an inhibitory effect on performance.

The Ethiopian, Abebe Bikila, after winning the Olympic marathon in 1960 continued on a lap of honour then at one point lay down on the ground to do some exercises, cycling in air, and the like. This was taken by the commentator on television to be a sign of his freshness. He was apparently showing off to the world that he had won with consummate ease and was suffering no ill effects. What he was doing, however, was eminently sensible.

3.21 Fainting after Heavy Exercise

If you stop suddenly at the end of an exhausting race or training session you may suffer slight dizziness or light-headedness. This is due to a shortage of oxygen supplied to the brain, usually caused by the reduction of blood pressure to the brain. Fainting is a reflex.

What causes this? Well, during heavy exercise blood is pumping around the body at a phenomenal rate, as high as 40 litres a minute in trained endurance athletes. A rate high enough to fill a car with petrol in one minute! Your muscles assist your heart in this task of pumping blood around your body because, by their tensing, they squeeze the veins that transport used blood back to the heart. As the veins are made up of hundreds of consecutive valves the blood can only flow in one direction along veins. Thus when the muscles relax, used blood, without oxygen, but carrying carbon dioxide, enters the veins only to be squeezed out again in the direction of the heart when the muscles contract.

This muscle pump helps to keep up the blood pressure on the inlet side of the heart so it does not have to do so much work to create the necessary blood pressure at the outlet side.

When you stop exercising, the muscle pump stops, the muscles relax but they are still screaming out for oxygen and there are still waste products such as carbon dioxide and lactic acid to be carried away. The heart now has to produce the required blood pressure without the help of the muscle pump. Blood pressure falls and the supply of blood and also oxygen to the brain falls causing a tendency to faint.

What happens next is that you panic and probably hyperventilate - breathe too fast. This has the effect of blowing off carbon dioxide, which is one of the stimuli to the heart so the heart rate drops and blood pressure drops further.

All that is necessary to prevent this sequence of events is to continue moving your muscles. It is not actually necessary to move your limbs as long as you keep the muscle pump going by alternately tensing and relaxing the muscles. The leg muscles are particularly valuable in this, as they are so large and can pump so much blood.

Soldiers standing still on parade for long periods use this technique to prevent fainting.

Lying down and cycling in the air is a particularly good way of preventing fainting. Perhaps this is what Abebe Bikila was up to.

3.22 How to Undertake Conditioning

There are three fundamental principles for getting into condition.

Take it easy at first. Low quality, low quantity. Light loads, low repetitions.

Progress from a broad range of movements towards the specific movements demanded by your sport.

Warm up before working hard.

3.23 Staying in the Game

When you are in good condition for harder training in a particular activity REMEMBER that you are not necessarily in good condition for other activities and that conditioning takes time.

Try to avoid repeated eccentric muscle contractions until you have achieved some level of conditioning.

Watch out for signs of illness and **do not train or compete if you have a temperature**.

As we have already covered warming up let's look a little more closely at the first principles of conditioning.

3.24 Take It Easy

"Walk and talk, jog and chat" summarises this point.

As far as aerobic conditioning is concerned, if you are out of breath to the point where you cannot talk then it is too hard for you. When you are training hard, as opposed to conditioning, then that is another matter. If you are not out of breath to the point where you cannot talk then your training may not be hard enough! That does depend though on the intended intensity of the training.

When it comes to strength or speed training different criteria have to be used. To say you should not lift a weight that you cannot lift 50 times assumes that you know what weight you can lift 50 times. If you do not know this and you have a go with a weight that you then find you can only lift 10 times then you have broken the "take it easy" rule straight away. Here common sense must prevail and the help and advice of a sympathetic coach or trainer should prove useful. In recruiting a coach you must make it quite clear at the outset that you are trying to get into condition for training and that you are not intent on breaking any world records until you are good and ready. Stop as soon as you get any hint of pain or strain. Leave it until you are in good condition.

3.25 Broad to Specific

We will come across this principle again in other contexts. Here it means first of all get your body into a generally good all round condition before you start to tax any particular aspect of its capabilities. Start with a wide range of activities performed gently. These could include swimming, walking, canoeing, and jogging and cycling, callisthenics, rowing, aerobics, weight training (with light weights) and so forth. Trying to avoid, at first, activities involving open skills where you are not in control the whole time. This means not playing ball games at first. The reason for this is that even if you are out of condition, the motivation to get to the ball may drive you to stretch or twist hard before your body is ready to take the strain. You are likely to end up with a pulled muscle, a torn ligament or tendon, even possibly heart failure. Heart failure amongst middle-aged men playing squash is not uncommon.

So stick to closed skills that are entirely under your control, that you can repeat over and over until you get yourself in condition. Keep the variety of your exercises as high as possible at first. Keep the quality and quantity of any one activity low. Do not strain yourself with too much of any one thing - that comes later when you start **training.**

During this early period you can gradually increase the quality of what you do by increasing the speed at which you perform your various activities or by increasing the load if you are working against resistance. You can gradually increase the quantity of what you do by performing more repetitions or exercising for longer periods. You should notice a fairly quick improvement in your capacity during the early stages without having to try hard. Just doing something instead of nothing will have a training effect.

Whether you will ultimately be training for strength or endurance or for something in between, it is wise, at first, to condition yourself for everything.

When your overall condition is good, and this is a very subjective thing to assess, you can begin to narrow down your conditioning activities. You do more of the activity that you are ultimately aiming to compete in and you do less of the other activities. Note I do not recommend that you cut them out altogether. Probably only in the final stages of preparation for an important event might you consider training in the event alone. Perhaps not even then.

Activities outside of your specific training for an event form an important part of relaxation and **they should be performed in a relaxed way** because you will not be conditioned enough to perform them with the same vigour as you ultimately perform in your chosen sport.

Now we are getting closer to the rather indistinct border between conditioning and training.

Remember that if you want a long and happy career in sport you have to be in good physical condition before you train and compete. If you want to stay in the game and avoid injury then follow the guidelines I have laid down for you. You will then stand a much better chance.

4 TOP TECHNIQUE TIPS

There are fundamental principles, laws, which govern all movements and the mastery of them. Here I will give you an insight into the way skills are mastered and performance improved so that you will be able to analyse your own performance with greater understanding and make worthwhile judgements about what to do next.

4.1 Relaxed Technique

Without any improvement in your physical capacity to do work, that is without any physical training designed to get you fitter, you can improve your efficiency in movement by up to one third simply by familiarity with the technique you are using. When you have first learned a skill you are all fingers and thumbs. Your actions are jerky and your body is tense. Response times are slow because every movement involves calculations in the brain. Reflex paths have not yet been firmly established. Your muscles tend to work against each other instead of against the load, which they are trying to move in a carefully controlled path.

As you progress the muscles that have been opposing the desired motion become more relaxed allowing a greater, better, faster, stronger motion from the muscles that are supposed to be doing the work. This is what relaxed technique is about. It is not the state of mind. It is not about relaxed working muscles. It is about relaxed non-working muscles.

In many sports, movements are repeated cyclically with alternate work and rest for the muscles involved. Even if they are not regularly cyclic as in running, cycling, canoeing, rowing, swimming etc. there may still be irregularly alternating movements. Tension and relaxation, violent explosive movements, gentle flowing ones. Tennis, cricket, American football - most sports have this feature in common. In very few does one remain perfectly still and tense or still and relaxed for any length of time. Weight lifting and target shooting spring to mind as sports that fall into these latter categories.

If you tense muscles unnecessarily you are doing unnecessary work that will impair your efficiency. Tense muscles use energy and if they do not need to be tense then they should be relaxed. Moreover tense muscles squeeze the tiny blood vessels, the capillaries, preventing blood from entering the muscles and supplying them with oxygen. This means that the muscles have to work without oxygen, i.e. anaerobically. That is okay for a very short time, but for anything longer than 30 seconds it is not okay because the energy yielding process then begins to produce lactic acid as a by-product. Lactic acid inhibits contraction, produces pain and affects the accuracy of the information provided by proprioceptors to the central nervous system. So movements become unreliable.

Alternate tension and relaxation however has the advantage of squeezing out blood from the veins in the direction of the heart thereby aiding the flow of blood around the body. If relaxation does not occur when it should then endurance is reduced and technique will suffer.

So improved technique, improved efficiency and improved performance run side-by-side and early improvement in performance is usually rapid.

An interesting example demonstrating how familiarity gives rise to efficiency is that both Olympic medal cyclists and untrained people, when tested on a cycle ergometer, have the same mechanical efficiency at submaximal loads. That is to say that for a given work output their consumption of oxygen was the same. The exception to this, discovered in 1976 by Vokac and Rodahl was that Eskimos, who were totally unfamiliar with the bicycle, had a markedly higher oxygen uptake for a given workload than did their Caucasian counterparts. This was because their unfamiliarity with cycling led to unnecessary muscular tension, which reduced their efficiency so they needed more oxygen to produce a given amount of power on the cycle ergometer.

4.2 Feedback is the Key

So how do you go about improving your technique? If you refer back to the chapter on learning you'll find that I mentioned **feedback**, referred to in some text books as **knowledge of results, KR**. This is the key to improvement of technique so we will go into the subject more deeply. (Skip this technical bit if it scares you and go to the conclusion).

Fortunately for us, control engineers have done all the work for us and we need only look at some of the conclusions they have drawn about feedback systems, without having to go into all the complicated mathematics showing how they arrived at their conclusions.

First of all let me illustrate a simple feedback system so that you get the idea of what they are. One that is familiar to all of us is the thermostatic control of temperature.

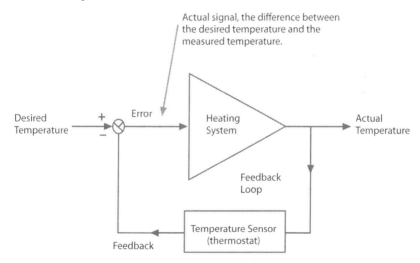

Figure 4.1

We know the temperature sensor as a thermostat, a simple on/off switch operated by the temperature that is being controlled. If the actual temperature is too low the thermostat detects this and the heater is switched on. When the actual temperature reaches the desired temperature then there is no error so the heater is switched off.

Desired Temperature - Actual Temperature = Error

When a positive error exists the heater is switched on. When the error is zero the heater is switched off.

This is a simple negative feedback system. Negative because the output of the system is subtracted from the input of the system to provide the actuating signal.

The ideal response from a system is that the actual output should exactly follow desired output. Thus if there is a sudden change in the input, with the ideal system there would also be a sudden change in the output of exactly the right magnitude.

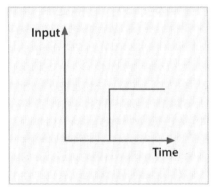

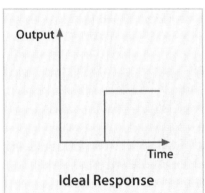

Ideal Response

Figure 4.2

If we look again at our heating system we see that the ideal response is impossible. It takes time to heat up a cylinder of water or a room or a storage heater. So the response to our input signal, the desired temperature, would be something like this.

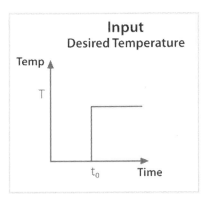

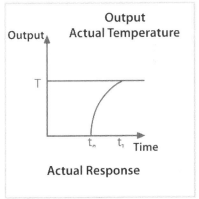

Figure 4.3

At time t_1 the required temperature T is reached and the heating system switches off.

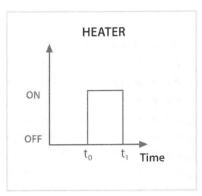

Figure 4.4

The description of our simple feedback system is not yet complete. What happens now, of course, is that some heat is gradually lost and the temperature falls. At some lower temperature T_1 depending on the sensitivity of the thermostat the heater is re-activated to raise the output temperature again. Here our system is displaying one of the key properties of negative feedback systems, that of regulation.

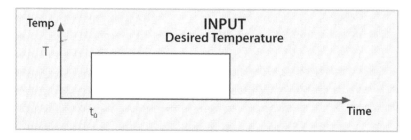

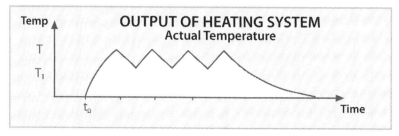

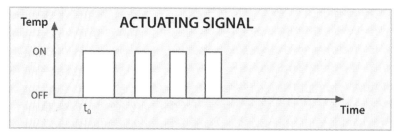

Figure 4.5

If the temperature falls from the desired temperature T to T_1 then the feedback system turns on the heater again.

The body has a temperature control system much like this but it operates on the blood vessels close to the surface of the skin, alternately opening and closing them so as to keep the core temperature constant.

4.2 Including People in the Loop

Many feedback systems include people in the feedback loop. Before we had thermostatically controlled central heating systems for our homes we simply had open fires. If we were too cold we lit a fire. If we got too hot we might open a window to let some heat out or simply allow the fire to subside. If we then became too cold we would put more coal on the fire. It soon became apparent that we could control the fierceness of a fire by controlling the amount of air that it has available to it. Thus most open fires have some way of opening and closing an air vent underneath the coal so as to allow more or less air through the fire. Nowadays modern coal-fired boilers can exclude the human from the feedback loop. Feedback systems within the boiler detect the temperature of the fire and the temperature of the system (water cylinder or room) being controlled. They then alter the amount of fuel being burned and its rate of burning automatically.

Returning briefly to sport we see that human beings can enter the feedback loop in many ways. The desired output might be to lift 100kg ten times in 30 seconds. Your body's own internal feedback systems control the execution of the lift. Outside of these internal feedback loops you may observe yourself in a mirror and outside of that your coach may be observing you and feeding back information on various matters. These may include technique but they may also include training. Suppose you fail to achieve the required result. The feedback that your coach may give you, so as to help your actual output become equal your desired output, might be that in order to achieve this "zero error" state you need more training of a particular type.

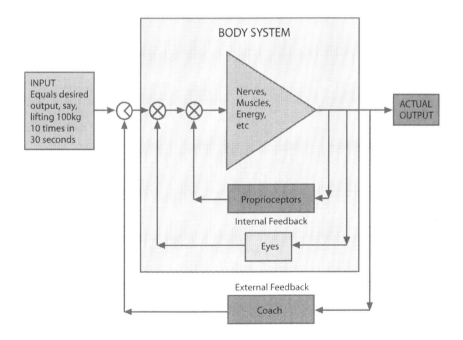

Figure 4.6

Of course, even this diagram is a gross over simplification of the actual feedback systems involved. You can add loop after loop after loop including the feedback from spectators, from your ears, from selectors, from video recordings. Feedback can be immediate or delayed, conscious or subconscious, good or bad quality, positive or negative. Looking within the body at your own internal feedback systems it confounds understanding if you consider that each nerve cell in the body may be in contact with as many as 200,000 other nerve cells. It has been estimated that one part of the brain associated with movement, known as the pyramidal tract, contains about 1.2 million nerve fibres in humans. You begin to comprehend the complexity of the control system that is the human being. However, despite this awesome complexity it is still possible to detect responses which, from control theory, we know are typical of much simpler control systems that are well understood.

4.3 Quality Feedback is Essential
Look at the simple feedback loop shown below.

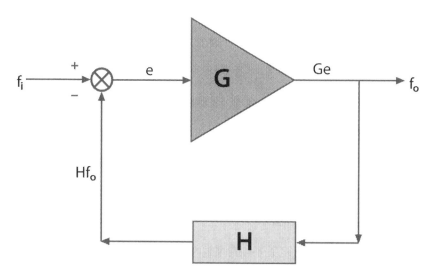

Figure 4.7

The symbols used are those conventionally used in control theory. If the following mathematics frightens you, **skip it** and go straight to 4.4, the **conclusion**.

The output f_o is equal to the error signal, e, times the gain, G.

$f_o = G.e$

And the proportion of the output fed back is the fraction H times the output f_o i.e. $H.f_o$. As this is subtracted from the input we get

$e = f_i - H.f_o$

If we now substitute this value of e in equation 1 we get

$f_o = G(f_i - H.f_o)$

Dividing both sides of equation 3 by f_i we get

$$f_o / f_i \qquad = G(1 - H.f_o / f_i)$$

$$= G - GHf_o / f_i$$

$$f_o / f_i + GHf_o / f_i = G$$

$$(1 + GH) f_o / f_i = G$$

$$f_o / f_i = G / (1 + GH)$$

Now if GH is very much greater than 1 then this equation approximates to

$$f_o / f_i = G/GH = 1/H$$

4.4 Conclusion

If the "open loop" gain, GH, is very much greater than 1 the output is independent of the gain of the system, G. What really determines the ratio of output to input now is the feedback factor, H, and NOT the gain, G. If the gain, G, varies with time this will not unduly affect the "closed loop" gain of the system f_o/f_i as long as the feedback factor remains constant.

What does this mean for you?

Well, so as far as the quality of your sports performance is concerned the quality of the feedback, which you receive, is of paramount importance!

A very simple example of this is the fact that good coaches get better results with their prodigies than bad coaches. It follows too that your performance will be limited if your coach, who provides you with external feedback, has limited ability.

Similarly the quality of the information obtainable from a video or a photograph affects the quality of your subsequent performance. If the quality of reproduction is not adequate for you to observe important details then you cannot feed back information on those details and no improvement can be made. Logical really.

The usefulness of the observation of bystanders will depend upon the quality of those observations. You can, of course, filter out those comments you do not wish to have fed back, disregarding the opinions of those whom you have no reason to respect and heeding the opinions of those whom you do respect. However, it is difficult to prevent harmful feedback from filtering through to the subconscious, which is a good reason for not reading press reports about yourself unless some trustworthy aide has first censored them.

4.5 Damped Responses

We used dampers in car suspension and pianos. They damp down oscillations, deaden vibrations or shock. Suppose a car goes over a sharp bump, equivalent to a step input to the car suspension system. The car, because it is suspended on springs, will tend to oscillate up and down.

Figure 4.8

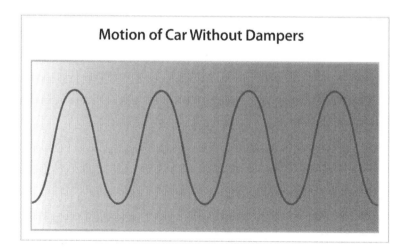

Figure 4.9

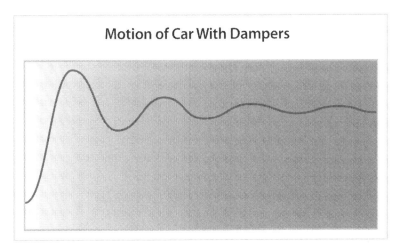

Motion of Car With Dampers

Figure 4.10

Dampers on cars are often referred to as shock absorbers.

The response of a piano string is much the same. When you strike a piano key the damper (a felt pad) is lifted off the string allowing it to vibrate freely. As soon as you release the piano key the damper comes into contact with the string again and damps out the oscillation.

4.6 Control Systems with Various Degrees of Damping

The response of control systems varies according to the type of feedback and the amount of feedback. Illustrated below are standard responses from feedback systems with varying degrees of damping, indicated by the damping factor.

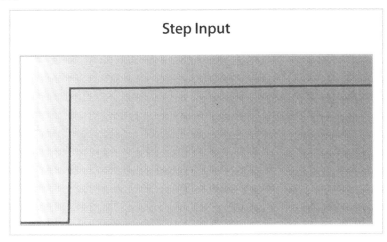

Step Input

Figure 4.11a

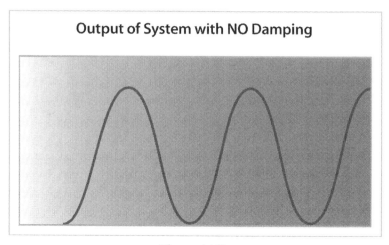

Figure 4.11b

Where do these typical systems responses occur in sport? Let me to give you some examples. An archer aims for a bull's eye and finds his arrow lands below the target so he aims higher next time. Then his next arrow lands too high. He has over corrected so next time he aims lower. This time he is below the target again but not as far as the first time. This archer is displaying the response of the under-damped system shown in figure 4.11c.

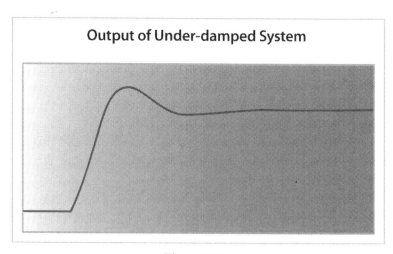

Figure 4.11c

His colleague also aims too low first time and raises his bow for the second shot. He under corrects, though, and finds his arrow closer to the target but still below. He continues aiming slightly higher each time until eventually he is on target. He is displaying the response of an over-damped system such as is depicted in figure 4.11d.

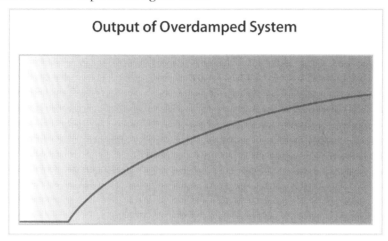

Figure 4.11d

A third archer (probably from South Korea!) misses first time but makes exactly the right correction and hits the bull's eye on her second attempt. She is displaying a critically damped response (Fig 4.11e) to the error signal that is actuating her motion.

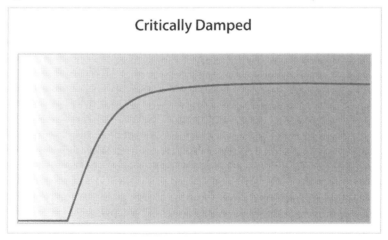

Figure 4.11e

This archer example is somewhat contrived, simply to illustrate the point that there is a feedback control system in operation here. The point worth noting is that if you have a tendency to over react then you are under-damped and will probably over-do your compensation or correction. Another example might be a gymnast's over-rotating in a backward somersault. Once realising or being told this, the under-damped gymnasts will have a tendency to under-rotate the next time and any coach or supporter should be ready for this. However, the over-damped gymnasts will continue to over-rotate on the next attempt but not by as much as the first time.

As your skill improves you become better able to control the damping factor, getting it nearer and nearer to 1 so that it becomes easier for you to learn new skills, especially ones that are closely related to what you already know.

The fact that the damping factor can come under your control is important to realise. The archery examples given above take no account of the fact that an under-damped archer can realise that he is over correcting and start to under correct like the over-damped archer. Or he may get his damping just right and hit the bull's eye next shot.

Whatever he does he is struggling to fine tune his feedback systems so that the error becomes zero as soon as possible.

4.7 What Controls the Damping Factor?

If I blindfold you and tell you to run along a path until you get to the finishing tape stretched across the path, you will not know that you have reached the tape until you touch it, so you will inevitably run through it. If I want you to stop at the tape I have to take off the blindfold so that you can not only detect where the tape is but how fast you are approaching it.

Your eyes provide you with two types of feedback, one is positional feedback and the other is velocity feedback. This velocity feedback is essential for accurate, quick control of position. Similarly, knowledge of acceleration is essential for accurate and quick control and alteration of velocity. In other words we control damping by feeding back not only the output but also the rate of change of the output.

This extra information improves the goodness of the system.

One example of how extra information of this sort can help athletes might be observed in rowing where the rowers are effectively blindfold because they are facing backward and cannot see the finish, nor any opposing crews that may be ahead of them. Here, the cox is the essential link in the feedback loop as it is the cox who can see what is going on and must relay information to the crew. If the cox simply says, "We are losing, go faster!" the crew will not find this particularly helpful. If the cox says, "We are two lengths behind the leaders and half a length down on the second crew with 500m to go. The second crew was 3/4 of length ahead when we had 750m to go so we can beat them." then the crew will find this information much more useful and encouraging. They know that they have little chance of winning but a good chance of getting a silver medal because at the current rate of progress they should be level with the crew ahead by the time they reach the finish.

The cox has provided information on position and the rate of change of position, the velocity, and thus has provided the necessary feedback for the crew critically to damp their response to his instruction to go faster. Without this essential feedback the crew would not know exactly what its response should be. Some members of the crew might panic and attempt to go too fast too soon, burning up their resources before the finish. Other members of the crew might over estimate the distance left to row or underestimate how far ahead the opposition might be. Either way they could find themselves on the finish line with energy to spare.

4.8 Stable and Unstable Systems

In a negative feedback system any disturbance to the system creates a disturbed output but this creates an error which the system corrects. If you draw hot water from your thermostatically controlled cylinder, which is replaced by cold water, the temperature will fall. The thermostat will detect this fall in temperature and switch on the heater thereby restoring the temperature to the desired value.

If the wind deflects the path of the archer's arrow, the archer will compensate for this by aiming slightly up wind.

In a stable system any oscillations that arise as a result of a disturbance will be damped out.

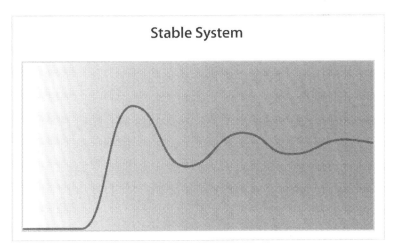

Figure 4.12

In an unstable system a small disturbance leads to oscillations that grow.

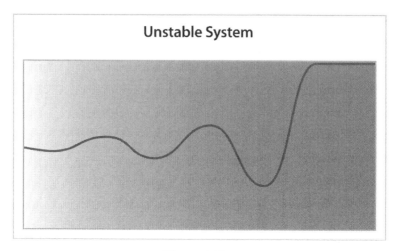

Unstable System

Figure 4.13

An example of this might be a gymnast attempting to balance on a beam. The oscillations cannot go on increasing to infinity and in practise they eventually reach a limit; in the case of the gymnast, when she falls of the beam.

The learner driver's kangaroo start is another example of a negative feedback loop giving rise to oscillations.

Control engineers know that if a system is unstable in this way it can be brought under control by increasing the amount of damping, or perhaps by putting an extra negative feedback loop around it. Control engineers have as many solutions as there are problems.

When you are learning or trying to improve skills it is the refinement of the feedback control systems that you are working on.

4.9 Delay in Feedback

One of the biggest problems that control engineers have to work with is delay. A large steel mill or chemical plant, for example, can have huge delays built into the system. One incorrect input at some essential stage could produce an error in the output that is not detected for some hours and a correction then would be too late to save vast amounts of waste, both in time and materials. Consequently the design engineers need to know their systems very well and build into them methods of error correction at every possible stage along the way.

You too can be spoiled in a similar way at an early stage in your development and much time and effort can be wasted if every stage of your development is not carefully monitored. If you are going to realise your ultimate potential you must have early errors corrected because, as I mentioned in Chapter 2, **"GOOD & BAD HABITS"** a fault once learned is almost impossible to eradicate. Also if you are ever over-faced, that fear in your subconscious can ruin your future and it may take you years to realise that you have been over-faced.

4.10 Video Recordings

On a shorter time scale you can experience delay in the feedback of information that could be of help to you. If you have had first-hand experience of videos as opposed to films you will realise the importance and value of video recordings. Films used to take weeks or months to come back from the developers and were more of a historical record than feedback. The information they contained was out of date and not as great in value as the information in a video recording which can be viewed immediately and corrective action taken straight away. Whilst you are learning a skill and all the reflexes are being established and feedback loops are being finely tuned you have a far better chance of extra feedback in the form of videos making an impact on your performance. Once the skill is established and learned, the feedback, whilst containing as much information, has lost a great deal of its effectiveness by delay. So don't delay, watch feedback straight away.

Mirrors in which you can watch your execution of a particular skill have some advantage over videos in the immediacy of the feedback they provide. There is no time delay. This is real time feedback, the best type. There is no problem with the image being reversed because we have all learned at an early age to cope with this. Indeed it is confusing to watch yourself on a TV monitor as the movements appear to be transposed left to right. Of course once you have mastered your skill you have to do without the mirrors so you have to learn to monitor internal forms of feedback.

4.11 Intrinsic Feedback

Whilst coaches, video recordings and the comments of interested observers can provide you with extrinsic feedback there is at great deal of information that is available to you internally. Intrinsic feedback falls neatly into two categories, that of the subconscious and that of the conscious. The highly skilled performer can bring subconscious feedback to consciousness to help improve skill. I will give you some examples of this and you will realise just how easy it is to do this and if you train yourself to do it you will undoubtedly improve.

Subconscious feedback comes from a multitude of sensors around the body known as receptors. They monitor temperature, pressure, position, speed, chemical concentrations, all manner of things. These receptors are positioned in muscles, ligaments, tendons, blood vessels, the skin, everywhere and there is a constant flow of information from them which is either acted upon or ignored as the case may be. The whole array forms part of an extremely complicated control system that is designed not only to perform accurately the tasks demanded of it by the brain but also to keep you alive by regulating things such as acid balance and temperature.

Conscious feedback you are aware of. Things that you can detect with the five senses, sight, hearing, smell, taste and touch provide information about which you are conscious usually. Sometimes though you see without noticing or hear without listening, touch without feeling.

As a performer you must learn to use all your senses to build up a picture of what it is that you are doing. You must feedback as much information as possible via the conscious mind.

It works like this. You latch onto something that should or should not be happening; something that you can readily observe but have never taken much notice of before. You observe this parameter of your performance and alter your performance so that the outcome of your actions is an improvement. You practise until you no longer need to observe the parameter because your new, improved skill has become ingrained in the subconscious.

To put it in another way, you use a special form of feedback that was always available but never used before to improve your technique. Then when you have improved your technique you relegate that feedback loop to the subconscious, using it consciously only now and again to make sure that your technique has not deteriorated.

Look

An example of this from sculling might be the observation of the wake left behind the boat. It is always there to be seen but it is more obvious in very calm conditions. One day you realise that if your sculling rhythm is erratic the wake reflects this and varies in width. So you start to monitor the wake and attempt to scull in such a way as to minimise the variation in width. You do this because you know that wide variations in speed during the sculling cycle are undesirable and inefficient. After some time you end up adapting your sculling technique so that each time you look at your wake you find it is now unvarying in width. You have achieved your objective and because your skill is now ingrained you no longer need to observe the wake so you relegate this feedback loop to the subconscious.

You have brought a subconscious feedback parameter to consciousness used it to improve your technique and then put it back again.

Listen

The sounds made in athletic or gymnastic movements can be very helpful in improving your technique. As a triple jumper you listen to the sounds your feet make each time they land and compare them with the rhythm that other top class athletes make. As you can hear frequencies up to 20kHz you should be able to detect time periods that are different by as little as 1/10,000th of a second. Your ears are therefore a great asset in providing detailed information about your movements. You can train yourself to compare consciously the period between takeoff and hop with the period between the hop and the step and the period between the step and the landing.

Similarly in gymnastics floor routines one of the images you should plant in your mind before a run is the anticipated rhythm of sounds from your various landings:- feet, hands, feet, hands, feet.......feet. Then compare this with the sounds you actually make. Later when you have mastered your routine you'll find that this particular feedback loop has been relegated to the subconscious. It is still there but you no longer have to concentrate on it.

Monitor Heart Rate

Your pulse rate is a very important indicator of your condition. Unfortunately it is affected by a great many things so you need to know what is normal and what is not normal if you want to be able to draw any useful conclusions from taking your pulse. For example you should be aware that if a member of the opposite sex takes your pulse it is likely to be higher than if you take it yourself.

Get used to taking your pulse at all times of the day and night, before, during and after exercise, sitting, standing, lying down, when you are well and when you are ill. Sitting here writing this, mine is 54. What is yours?

One day at a very important event my pulse rate never dropped below 100 even though I had an hour to recover between each of three heats and a final. This indicated a high state of arousal. The fact that I spent half the day on the toilet was another indicator!

On another occasion I was able to use my pulse to calm myself when I was over excited about an important race. I will refer to arousal in the chapter on Psychology – MIND YOUR HEAD.

You can and should monitor your recovery from exercise with your pulse rate. This subject I will cover more fully in Physical Training. You can also monitor the intensity of your training effort this way.

Feel

In every sport you make contacts. You touch your equipment or the ground or an opponent or team-mate. In some you sit. In others you lie down. Every conceivable position is encountered in sport. But when you touch, do you feel? Are you aware of the exact part your body that is making contact? Are you aware of the length of time that you are in contact? What pressure do you feel when you are in contact? Does the pressure vary? Should it vary? As an exercise, list the points of contact that you make in your sport and ask yourself these questions about them. Make yourself more aware of what you are doing. Give yourself alternative feedback paths to monitor and I guarantee you will improve as a result.

4.12 Fault Correction

So my advice has come too late for you and you have developed the fault in your technique that you do not seem to be able to eradicate. This is what you do.

Start again!

As it is virtually impossible to unlearn a skill, what you have to do is learn another skill, the correct one this time. You have heard it many times I feel sure - "Back to Basics". You simply go back to the beginning as though you were learning a new sport and work through the recognised progressions. There will come a point where your fault will try to creep back in and at this point you must breakdown the progression into smaller bits, practising each bit until it is mastered. Eventually you will have mastered the complete skill in its correct form and if you continue to practise correctly then you will "make perfect".

Simple when you know how, is it not?

Yet how many coaches do you see struggling on with athletes performing badly, simply giving them external feedback in the hope that the fault can be corrected? Once a fault is badly entrenched it is too late for feedback. You simply have to start again.

Actually, it is not always necessary to go right back to the very beginning. Often you can spot where in the cycle of events that make up your skill it is breaking down. Take a simple, 10-bounce, trampoline routine. The seventh bounce may be a front somersault which you can do perfectly well on its own but in this routine you fluff it and that puts you wrong for the eighth, ninth and tenth bounces. The fault probably does not even lie in the somersault itself. It is most likely to be in the move before. So you practice the move before and get it right eventually. Then you put the two together. Then you put the move after the somersault in as well, because up to now you have not practised that correctly. Eventually you piece together your routine and then you get to the sixth bounce, hey presto, you do it correctly, and surprise, surprise your landing sets you up perfectly for the somersault that is now no problem at all and the remainder of the routine falls into place.

4.13 Compete, Compete, Compete

It is no use becoming the best practice player in the world. A training champion. The only way that you can prove you are the best is to compete. But competition is a skill in itself that has to be learned. There are rules to be understood and complied with, tactics to be learned, different venues with which you need to become familiar, many mistakes from which to learn along the road to success.

It is far better to make your mistakes as a novice when the result is not that important than it is to make a novice's error in the Olympic final. You do not want to end up watching your Olympic final, the one you should be in, on television in the Olympic Village simply because you cannot understand a 24-hour clock. This actually happened to two American sprinters in the Munich Olympics because they thought that 15:00 hours was 5 o'clock.

You do not want to be disqualified for a rule violation that you never heard about. It happens in novice events all the time but this is how you learn. Far better then than at the world championships.

I did not include this section in the chapter on learning because it is more important to learn good technique than to compete. During competition technique often deteriorates and this can impede progress instead of aiding it. However, once you have reached a certain stage it is important to place yourself under the stress of competition because this stress often leads to technical breakdown. This will then give you something more to work on in your training. Just when you thought you had got your sport worked out you find that under stress you have a problem. Remember that the competition situation is often quite different to the training situation and so it is important to expose yourself to it.

4.14 Get Used to Losing

This may seem an odd thing to say in a book about winning. But the odds are stacked against your winning all the time so you had better get used to losing. If on average there are eight people competing in your category then every eighth event you should win if you are at a similar standard. If you win more frequently than that then you are too good and in most sports you will find yourself promoted to a class where you do not find it so easy. If you find that you are not winning every eighth event then you are not good enough and need to improve. Of course, the bigger the field the less likely you are to win.

As long as you feel you are in with a good chance you will enjoy your sport and losing will not disappoint you too much. But lose you will, so you must learn to accept defeat with good grace.

If you hide yourself away and practice until you are much better than the opposition in your class, so that you only ever win, you run the risk of the becoming contemptuous of other competitors. Then when you do lose you will not know how to cope with the failure. Remember that without losers there would be no winners, indeed no competition.

Winning or losing by a large margin is not nearly a satisfying as participating in a closely fought competition, whether you win or lose. Spectators prefer close competitions too. So compete at your own level.

Pierre de Coubertin said it all in his speech at a banquet for Olympic officials on the 24th July 1908 "... the important thing in life is not victory but

the struggle; the essential thing is not to have won but to have fought well...".
It irks me that this speech is so often misquoted as, "... it is not the winning
but the taking part that counts...".

4.15 Equipment

Your sports equipment should become like an extension to your body.
Without looking you should be able to place it accurately to within
millimetres of where you want it. A squash player should seldom hit the wall
with the racket. An oarsman should be able to keep an oar millimetres off the
water, without touching, during the recovery phase of the stroke. A horse
rider should be able to feel when the horse is standing exactly square without
looking to see if a leg is misplaced forward or backward. The skier should
know as soon as the skis are put on whether the balance is correct. The tennis
player should be able to feel a string loosening in the racket. Only years of
practice and experience will teach you these skills. To acquire that sensitivity
takes a very long time. When you have become sensitive, only the best will do.
Only the highest manufacturing standards will satisfy you and your sport
becomes rather expensive.

The obsession that many top sports performers have with the quality of
their equipment manifests itself in different ways. Logically if you have an
item of equipment with which you are totally familiar and you know exactly
how it responds in every situation then it makes sense to hang onto it and not
to change it in anyway. That is of course unless you are dissatisfied with it in
some way. Ivan Lendl changed his tennis racket several times in one tennis
match! I can only assume that like tennis balls his rackets changed their
characteristics after a fairly short period and he was so sensitive to this that he
demanded a new racket with considerable frequency. This is okay if you can
afford it. On the other hand, of course, one does not observe this behaviour
with other tennis players.

In a borrowed boat I once experienced the perfect sculling moment. This
boat was so comfortable that I felt totally secure and I could go faster and
faster simply by pushing harder and harder with my legs as though I was
sitting on a leg press machine. No matter what I did there was no tendency
for the boat to become unstable. I have been searching for that perfect rig in
a sculling boat ever since. I had thought it would be fairly easy to recreate it in
another boat but the feeling eluded me. So I bought the best boat I could lay
my hands on and still I could not get the same feeling of security and
comfort. I have become renowned for fiddling with my equipment in the
seemingly futile search for this perfect rig. It has become for me like Sullivan's
"Lost Chord" on the Organ.

I have this pernickety, fiddly nature in common with Perti Karpinen who
has several times been Olympic Sculling Champion. I understand that he too
used to spend a lot of time making fine adjustments to his boat. On the other

hand Chris Ballieu and Alan Whitwell, two of Britain's top scullers in the eighties, did not adjust their equipment from one end of the year to another if they could avoid it.

I was once observed a sculler who went on to become junior national champion sculling with the most appalling technique quite clearly brought about by poorly adjusted equipment. His blade work was good and he obviously went fast but he could have gone faster if he had not had to use his muscles to compensate for the imperfections in his boat and sculls. This is not to say that he would have gone faster with well-rigged equipment straight away. Chances are that he would have gone slower initially because the rig would have felt unnatural to him. He had learned to scull his boat rig exceptionally well and a skill once learned and ingrained cannot be unlearned just like that. He would have had to start again learning a new technique with a new boat.

I remember, myself, being very disappointed not to find myself going any faster in my own new boat when I bought it.

I think that my fussiness and perhaps that of Karpinen have come about because I experienced a well rigged boat at a stage in my own development when I was not good enough to be able to detect any imperfections that there may have been in it. Now, with many more years' experience, my standards are inevitably higher and it is impossible to find a rig that can satisfy me in the same way. It appears I must die frustrated.

Pre-Competition Adjustments

I cannot, in all honesty, recommend that you make out of the ordinary adjustments "no matter how small" to your equipment, just before a competition. The temptation is all too great, I know. That niggling little irregularity that you have suffered throughout your training now seems to loom large and threatens your chances of winning that important event. So at the last minute you think you will try something. A new bit for your horse's mouth, half a degree of extra castor on a racing car wheel, a different handgrip on your fencing rapier, longer or shorter spikes in your shoes. The list of possible permutations in each sport is endless. DON'T DO IT. If you are going to make changes, do them in training and in plenty of time. My own experience tells me that the last-minute alteration is seldom if ever effective. You perform better with imperfect but familiar equipment than you do with perfect but unfamiliar equipment. And of course there is always the chance that the alteration you make is not an improvement at all. Then you are doubly handicapped.

A recent British lightweight women's coxless four had five different gearing permutations for different wind conditions. But they had all been tried out and practised with beforehand. Now that is what I call thorough preparation.

4.16 Do Not Accept the Obvious

Improvements in performance over the years have often been due to improvements in equipment or technique brought about by being different. The most obvious example of this has to be the invention of the high jumping technique known as the Fosbury Flop. Up until 1968 almost every high jumper had to accept that the straddle technique was the ultimate style for high jumping. The technique involved facing downward while jumping over the bar in what would be termed a forward motion. Dick Fosbury won the Olympic title in Mexico, turning everything that was conventional about high jumping upside down. He jumped backwards over the bar, facing towards the sky as he went. He did not, however, break the world record at the time and both straddlers and Fosbury floppers held the world record over the ensuing years until the flop technique established itself as the superior way of jumping.

What Dick Fosbury did was a bit of lateral thinking. Whilst everybody else was playing Follow the Leader, Dick Fosbury played "What if?" "What if I jumped backwards?" He did not accept what was obvious.

The invention of the butterfly stroke was another creation of an imaginative person performing "Operation Zig Zag". You examine what everybody else is doing, establish the norm and then do something different. When they Zig you Zag. In the case of butterfly the novelty was the out of the water recovery of the arms which until then in " breast stroke" had been done under the water. Unfortunately the advantage of this technique over the traditional breast stroke was so great that it became a banned technique for breast stroke and was introduced as a style in its own right. This was a very reasonable course of action for the swimming authorities to take, given the speed and attractiveness of the new style to swimmers at large.

Progress in swimming technique since has been limited somewhat to such small items as the number of leg beats employed per arm stroke.

Progress in high jumping has moved side-by-side with improvements in the softness and safety of the landing area. Clearly the Fosbury flop would have been unthinkable into a sandpit.

In rowing it was known that a narrow, long boat incurred less water resistance than a wide, short boat but the narrowness was limited by the distance that the oarlock had to be from the rower to provide the correct leverage for the oar. Suddenly somebody hit on the idea of an outrigger that allowed the oarlock to be placed outside the boat instead of in the gunwale where it had traditionally been placed for centuries. Immediately it was possible to build much narrower and faster boats.

Another example of the Zagging instead of Zigging in rowing came with the introduction of the sliding outrigger in place of the sliding seat in the early 1980s. This had the advantage of reducing the cyclic variations in the speed of the boat each stroke. The International Rowing Federation decided in this case to nip the idea in the bud because of the expense that would be incurred worldwide in a sport which was already considered expensive. It was felt that the technologically-advanced, wealthier nations of the first world would have had an unfair advantage over the developing nations who were just beginning to make some headway in the sport.

Bear in mind, when you develop a new idea as a result of not accepting the obvious, you are likely initially to regress in your performance as you will have to acquire a new skill with all that this entails. Do not be discouraged from your idea though if it is based on well founded principles. I could never understand the benefit of a hitch kick in the long jump. Now I observe athletes simply hanging in the air, which seems to me to be both simpler and logical.

As I said before, progress in athletic performance often goes hand in hand with technological advances. I doubt whether today's gymnasts would be able to perform triple back somersaults without the aid of excellent sprung floors. Today's sophisticated vaults could not be undertaken if all that was available to aid flight in take off was a 1940s beat board.

Sports men and women often quickly take advantage of modern materials. In 1980s when carbon/kevlar was commonplace in racing boats I was surprised not yet to have seen a bicycle made almost entirely from the stuff, given the strength, stiffness and lightness of the material. Now, of course, it has all been done.

4.17 Developing Technical Exercises

In every sport there are technical exercises which have been developed over the years to aid participants in the learning of basic technique and in the further improvement of technique. These exercises usually take the form of a small part of the overall technique exaggerated in some way, so as to emphasise the coaching point, and then practised repeatedly until the exercise is mastered. Hopefully then the athlete is able to "carry over" the skill thus acquired in the exercise to the sport itself.

Examples of these exercises might be riding a horse without stirrups, rowing with only one hand on the oar handle, sprinting with exaggerated knee lifting, Kimiing in karate, swimming with feet only and so on. The examples are legion.

However well designed these exercises may be they are only exercises and as such they are skills which can be mastered with practice. Remember PERFECT PRACTICE MAKES PERFECT. The trick is in carrying over the correct practice of the exercise, often performed in an artificially created environment, to the sport in question when performed in the competitive situation. Sometimes the application of the newly acquired skill is easily made and immediate improvement in the overall skill is apparent. At other times the mental leap from the exercise to the full skill is too great for an individual and no improvement is made. Sometimes the "traditional" exercises will have no impact on your skill.

This is when your ability to be creative (not to accept the obvious) will set you apart from other athletes. There is no reason why you cannot invent technical exercises of your own to improve your skill. Often we are aware of an imperfection in our technique because of a perceptive comment made by an onlooker or because of a revealing photograph taken by friend. It could be a long-standing fault that you have never got to grips with. Now it is impeding your progress. This one problem may be what comes between you and that coveted gold medal. If only you could think of a way of curing it.

But you can. There are no such things as problems, only challenges. Problems are your opportunity to be creative. All you have to do is to think of an exercise that will help you to eliminate your fault. It may not be in any of the coaching manuals on your sport but if it works for you it is a perfectly valid exercise. Just examine the part of your skill that is faulty in fine detail and extract the tiniest part that you can so that you can practise it without the fault. You may have to create an artificial situation to do this. Here are some examples.

Practising with one hand at a time when normally both hands would have to work together.

Doing the exercise while stationary when the complete skill is performed on the move.

Getting through the action standing on your feet or sitting down when normally you would have to perform it upside down. Learning an Eskimo roll in a canoe is done this way at first.

Practising your skill in a stable situation when normally you would be required to perform it in an unstable situation.

Reducing the perceived risk, say by reducing the height at which you have to perform then reintroducing the risk by going back up to the normal height.

At this stage it does not matter that the exercise situation is artificial. All you are trying to do is eliminate your fault by learning your skill from scratch again but in an unconventional way.

The next steps are to add to your exercise what would normally precede your faulty (but now correct) movement and what would normally succeed the movement, first performing two movements slowly and deliberately and correctly then the three movements slowly and deliberately and correctly. You see that what you are doing is not one exercise but a series of exercises making up a learning progression.

The next stage is to improve the speed and consistency with which you undertake the one, two and three exercises or however many exercises you feel are necessary. After this you gradually reintroduced your normal environment. You might progress from a very stable situation to an unstable situation or from a stationary to a slow moving and then a fast-moving situation, from a safe to a dangerous situation. Take your skill forward in easy, logical, small steps, making sure that your fault does not reappear.

When you have made good progress you must then extend yourself. Take the skill to speeds that are beyond what you would normally experience so that normality falls well within your range of capabilities. Go much slower than normal as well as much faster than normal. Think of ways of making your skill more difficult to perform. Close your eyes, hold on with your fingernails, do it with hiking boots on, do it with no shoes on at all, do it on one leg. Stretch your skill to its limits so that the normal conventional skill with which others may still be struggling is a piece of cake to you.

4.18 Search for Efficiency

Almost all sports demand either speed or endurance in one way or another from the athlete. Your technique is obviously of paramount importance in improving your capacity to endure your sport or your capacity to move quickly. Efficiency plays a large part in this. You want as much of your energy expenditure as possible to go into improving your speed in the direction that is going to be of most value. If only a certain speed is required then the proper use of your available energy resources will enable you to endure your sport better and for longer.

Remember that there is a law of conservation of energy. When energy is used to perform work it simply changes its state and the total energy is conserved. Thus a falling weight transforms its "potential energy", due to its position and the force of gravity on it, into "kinetic energy" due to its velocity. The amount of potential energy lost in falling equals the amount of kinetic energy gained in the fall. When the weight eventually hits something and comes to rest the kinetic energy is converted into sound and heat energy. If you drop a weight into water, sound is created, heat is created and waves radiate out from the point of impact carrying energy in them.

In the search for efficiency in sport you should try not to make waves. Sounds you make on impact are sound waves that are wasted energy. If waves radiate out from your boat due to unnecessary vertical movements then you are losing energy to the outside world, which could be kept within the environment of you and your boat. If by your actions you create unnecessary friction you will heat up the environment wastefully. This is why you should clean and polish your equipment before competing if air or water friction is an important factor. Grease and oil moving parts that would otherwise have made it harder for you to move fast or which might prevent you from using relaxed technique.

Whilst it is not possible to apply this advice literally in all sports, the basic principle of efficiency in the use of your energy must always apply. In almost every case it is the direction of movement or the path of movement which is critical and it is the misdirection or the misapplication of force which leads to energy being misspent.

4.19 Two Biomechanical Laws

When working on your technique there are two fundamental biomechanical principles that should know about.

- The acceleration path should be as long as possible.
- There should be no unnecessary accelerations or decelerations in an athletic movement.

To illustrate these let me draw your attention to hammer throwing. It's not something most of us will ever have attempted. But you are sure to have seen it on TV. In order to increase the acceleration path and make it as long as possible the number of turns that hammer throwers make within the circle has increased over the years giving more time for acceleration and thus a greater final velocity at the release of the hammer.

Even modern shot putters have incorporated turns in the throwing circle rather than simply stepping backwards and turning.

Now imagine if a hammer thrower were to turn very quickly in the first turn and then slow down in the second turn and attempt to speed up again in the final turn(s). What would be the point of that? Or imagine a javelin thrower running up to the line as fast as possible and then slowing down and speeding up again before throwing. It takes effort to slow down and effort to speed up again. These are slightly outrageous examples in order to make a point but you can apply this law about unnecessary accelerations and decelerations to any part of any athletic movement. Bear it in mind.

5 OVERLOADED SUBMARINE

5.1   Stress and The Overload Principal
5.2   Strength
5.3   Speed or Acceleration
5.4   Fast Strength
5.5   Stamina or Endurance
5.6   The Middle Ground
5.7   Flexibility
5.8   The Basic Energy Systems
- ATP
- PC
  o   Sprinting
- Anaerobic Glycolysis
- Aerobic Metabolism
  o   The Submarine Analogy
5.9   Training - The Choice
5.10 General Principles of Training
- Broad to Specific
- Training Individual Parts
- Creative Overloading
- Specificity of Training

5.1 Stress and the Overload Principle
The body responds to stress like a spring. You push it down and it bounces back when you rest it. If you subject your body to stress it says to itself, "I didn't like that. I'd better do something so that next time it won't hurt so much". And so the body's damage control team turns to, repairing

here and reinforcing there so that, sure enough, the next time you subject your body to that stress it does not hurt as much. This is known as the "Training Result".

But then you fool your body by subjecting it to an even greater stress that hurts it just as much as the first time. So the body says, "Ha! Two can play at that game," and it makes even greater improvements.

Of course, the law of diminishing returns comes into play eventually. Initially, improvement is quick and substantial but the more you improve the more effort and pain is required to achieve only slight improvements. The body says, "Well there is not a lot I can do now in the way of adaptation and improvement so it is just jolly well going to have to hurt every time you do that". This is when athletes either injure themselves or turn to their equipment to see if there is anyway that they can go faster, jump higher, kick or throw further. Some, of course, turn to drugs but that is cheating and we don't do cheating.

Naturally whilst the body is undertaking repairs and renewals it must be rested. The mechanic cannot fix the racing car whilst it is out on the track. He has to wait until it comes into the pits. And if an engine needs to be rebuilt with structural changes then it may need to be off the road overnight or even for weeks.

You cannot keep depressing the spring without allowing it a chance to spring back up. See overtraining.

So in order to train your body and achieve the much sought-after "Training Result" you have to place it under stress and then **rest it**. It is as simple as that. And you achieve the stress by overloading the particular muscle or energy system that you wish to improve, that is to say by subjecting it to a load that is greater than it would normally experience. Because your body adapts to a particular workload you have to increase the overload progressively in order to achieve a steady improvement. Eventually improvements become more and more difficult to achieve because of the law of diminishing returns.

Consider this question. Do professional athletes perform better because they have more time to train or because they have more time to rest?

It is possible to pick any physical aspect of performance and train it this way so let us look at the basic aspects so that we know what we are training.

5.2 Strength

Your ability to apply great force with the muscles. This can include the strength of your heart muscle, which is trainable.

5.3 Speed or Acceleration

Your ability to execute a movement very fast. This is closely allied to strength but it is not the same.

5.4 Fast Strength

Your ability to move a load quickly. Sir Isaac Newton discovered the law relating force (strength) and acceleration and in a simplified form it says that the acceleration of a body is proportional to the force applied to it. Also that the smaller the mass of the body the greater will be its acceleration for any given force.

Force, F, equals mass, m, multiplied by acceleration, a.

$F = ma$

This means that the stronger you become the greater the weight to you can lift. It also means that you can lift a given weight faster if you are stronger. Obvious really. But it means that if your own weight stays constant and your strength improves then you should be able to move your own weight faster. So strength, acceleration, speed and mass are related.

5.5 Stamina or Endurance

Your ability to endure an activity for a lot of time. Again it is fairly obvious to most people that the harder you do something the shorter is the time you can endure doing it. Endurance activities are low in quality and high in quantity. Strength or speed based activities are the other way around.

5.6 The Middle Ground

Between speed and endurance there is this middle ground which places demands upon both strength and endurance. It is sometimes referred to as muscular endurance or speed endurance but neither of these terms describes it properly nor explains the special training required and the different physiological demands placed upon your body. To understand this middle ground fully you need to know something about how the body converts food (its fuel) into movement. I will tackle this shortly.

5.7 Flexibility

Some sports movements require incredible flexibility whilst others demand stability, immobility and rigidity in certain joints. It is a mistake to regard high levels of flexibility as a prerequisite for good performance in all sports.

5.8 The Basic Energy Systems
ATP

Muscular contraction uses the energy released when adenosine triphosphate, ATP, is converted into adenosine diphosphate, ADP. The energy released is exactly the right amount for contraction. The muscles have a ready supply of ATP in them that is always used first.

onlyIn fact the ATP -> ADP breakdown is the only energy source in immediate use by muscles. All other energy sources are used to rebuild the ATP molecules from ADP.

PC

Phosphocreatine is used to rebuild ATP in the simplest way by the creation of sufficient phosphate and energy when PC breaks down into creatine.

PC -> Pi + C + energy

Energy + ADP + Pi -> ATP

Whilst these equations are only simplified they demonstrate the end result. In actual fact the process requires the presence of enzymes. Ironically the only way that creatine can be returned to PC is by the breakdown of a molecule of ATP to ADP. This happens during the recovery from exercise when ATP is reformed from foodstuffs by other processes.

Sprinting

These two energy systems, the ATP and the PC systems, are the sprinters systems. The ATP will last for about two seconds and PC will last for about a further eight seconds. Both systems can really be lumped together in what is known as the phosphagen or ATP-PC system. The energy can be released very quickly but there is only a short supply of it. Oxygen is not required for the release of energy by the ATP-PC system so it is an anaerobic process (anaerobic meaning without air).

Anaerobic Glycolysis

After the ATP and the PC systems of energy release there is a third anaerobic process in which food, only in the form of glucose or glycogen (a polymer of glucose), is broken down to provide the energy for the resynthesis of ATP. The eventual by-product of this anaerobic glycolysis is lactic acid, which causes fatigue and eventually makes you stop working. By the time the concentration of lactic acid reaches intolerable levels the energy that has been made available by anaerobic glycolysis is about twice that which is available by the phosphagen system. This means that the lactic acid system, as it is often referred to, is of great importance in events such as 400m and 800m running. In fact any intense activity lasting between 15 seconds and 2-4 minutes relies heavily on the lactic acid system.

This is the middle ground, to which I referred before, that falls between the two stools of speed and endurance.

Aerobic Metabolism

The breakdown of food fuels with oxygen is known as aerobic metabolism and includes the aerobic breakdown of glycogen, aerobic glycolysis, as well as fat metabolism. To produce the same amount of energy slightly more oxygen is required (15 percent more) if fat is used as the fuel than if glycogen is used.

Obviously glycogen is therefore the preferred fuel. However there is not sufficient glycogen stored in the body for very long intensive exercise and after about two hours fat metabolism takes over from aerobic glycolysis. The body has enough fat stored for work measured in hundreds or thousands of hours because the amount of energy released by fat metabolism for the resynthesis of ATP is very substantial. Fat is an efficient store of energy.

The oxygen required for aerobic metabolism is provided by the oxygen transport system, the lungs, heart and blood. It takes a while for this oxygen transport system to respond to the stimulus of exercise and even then the rate of production of energy by the system is low compared with the anaerobic systems, too low for sprinting. However because of the substantial fuel supplies and their efficient use when broken down in the presence of oxygen the aerobic system is the preferred system for endurance activity.

The by-products of the aerobic metabolism are carbon dioxide and water. Carbon dioxide is transported via the bloodstream back to the lungs where it is expelled from the body. If demand for oxygen exceeds supply then anaerobic glycolysis takes place, lactic acid is produced and the work rate has to be lowered until supply equals demand.

The Submarine Analogy

Compare the energy systems of your body with those of a conventional submarine. The motor, which drives the submarine's propeller, is powered by electricity stored in batteries. This is equivalent to the phosphagen system because the supply of electricity is severely limited and the batteries have to be frequently re-charged. However the batteries do have the advantage that they do not require oxygen which enables the submarine to proceed underwater. Although they do not last long the batteries can provide substantial power and enable the submarine to sprint underwater. Obviously if a large amount of energy is used quickly in this way then the submarine has to surface more frequently to recharge its batteries. This would be equivalent to sprinting and then recovering, sprinting and then recovering, sprinting and then recovering.

To replenish the submarine's batteries a diesel powered electric generator is used. To burn the diesel the submarine has to surface or at least snorkel so that oxygen is available. This is equivalent to the aerobic process. With a large cargo of diesel and a limitless supply of air the submarine has considerable endurance when operating this way. The generator can re-charge the batteries continuously whilst the motor discharges them continuously. Eventually though the diesel might run out and then extra supplies (food) would be required.

The analogy can be extended a little further because within the muscles there is a small quantity of oxygen stored. The use of this equates to the submarine running its diesel whilst underwater but using up the air inside the submarine. Obviously this would not last long and neither does the oxygen stored in the muscles.

Here though the analogy breaks down somewhat because there is no real equivalent to the lactic acid or anaerobic glycolysis system. This is because diesel will not burn without oxygen. However, if it could, then the by-product of the release of energy from the incomplete combustion of diesel in the engine would quickly lead to the seizure of the engine, much as the by-product of anaerobic glycolysis, lactic acid leads to the seizure of the muscles.

5.9 Training - The Choice

You can train the phosphagen systems and the aerobic system but *according to Ulrich Hartman, the German physiologist, there is no evidence in any of the literature to suggest that it is possible to train the lactic acid or anaerobic glycolysis system.*

The duration of your event is the single most important factor in determining which energy system is used most and therefore what proportion of your training time you should spend on it. This seems an uncannily simple idea but it is amazing how many sports people get their training wrong because they either do not know this or they have not been able to bridge the gap between the traditional training methods and modern ones based on up-to-date scientific knowledge.

Clearly the oxygen uptake system is the predominant factor in the performance of endurance events such as the marathon. Here the main factor that requires training is a physiological parameter known as your maximum oxygen uptake or max VO_2. This is your aerobic power. Another important parameter for endurance is your anaerobic threshold, which is the percentage of your max VO_2 at which you can work without accumulation of lactic acid. This is especially important for very long endurance events but it has a bearing on all endurance events, even those as short as 6 minutes. Max VO_2 can be improved by around 20 percent in untrained subjects but if you are already training then your scope for improvement is reduced by the law of diminishing returns. On the other hand if you have been bedridden for any length of time your scope for improvement may be as high as 100 percent. You cannot, therefore, measure an athlete's max VO_2 and predict his/her ultimate potential with any reliability. No athlete can perform at their maximum aerobic power for very long because in order to achieve their maximum oxygen uptake they have to cross what is known as their anaerobic threshold. Once crossed they find that lactic acid is produced more quickly than the body can assimilate it and they are eventually forced to stop working. The closer the anaerobic threshold is to the max VO_2 the less lactic acid is produced and the better an athlete can perform. So there is still room for improvement by training in such a way as to increase the level of the anaerobic threshold, even when the max VO_2 can be improved no more.

At the other end of the scale are the explosive movements such as throwing, punching, jumping, lifting and sprinting. These all require strength, high power, great speed and often flexibility. The energy system used is the phosphagen system but the central nervous system requires training too. I'll show you how this is done.

In between we find events requiring a blend of all three systems - the phosphagen system, the lactic acid system and the oxygen system. The figures in table 5.1, below, show in what proportions. It is interesting to note that although it is possible to have requirements for almost 100 percent phosphagen or 100 percent oxygen systems, in no intermediate event is there ever a requirement for 100 percent lactic acid system.

Duration of Performance Min : Sec	Typical Event	ATP-PC System Strength/ Speed	Lactic Acid System Anaerobic Capacity	Oxygen System Aerobic Capacity
130:00-180:00	Marathon	-	5%	95%
30:00 - 50:00	10,000m	5%	15%	80%
13:00 - 25:00	5,000m	10%	20%	70%
8:00 - 14:00	3000m	20%	40%	40%
3:30 - 6:00	1500m	20%	55%	25%
1:40 - 2:45	800m	30%	65%	5%
0:45 - 1:20	400m	80%	15%	5%
0:20 - 0:35	200m	98%	2%	-
0:10 - 0:15	100m	98%	2%	-
0:00 - 0:03	Explosive	100%	-	-
Sports Examples				
Baseball		80%	20%	-
Basketball		85%	15%	-

Fencing		90%	10%	-
Hockey		60%	20%	20%
American Football		90%	10%	-
Golf		95%	-	5%
Gymnastics		90%	10%	-
Ice Hockey	a. Forwards/Defence	80%	20%	-
	b. Goalie	95%	5%	
Lacrosse	a. Goalie, defence, attack	80%	20%	
	b. Midfielders, man-down	60%	20%	20%
Rowing	a. 2000m	20%	30%	50%
	b. 1000m	20%	50%	30%
	c. 500m	30%	65%	5%
Rugby Football		80%	20%	-
Cricket		95%	5%	-
Skiing	a. Slalom, jumping, downhill	80%	20%	-
	b. Cross country	-	5%	95%
	c. Leisure Skiing	34%	33%	33%

Soccer	a. Goalie, wingers, strikers	80%	20%	-
	b. Midfield	60%	20%	20%
Swimming/ Diving	a. 50m, diving	98%	2%	-
	b. 100m	80%	15%	5%
	c. 200m	30%	65%	5%
	d. 400m	20%	40%	40%
	e. 1500m	10%	20%	70%
Tennis		70%	20%	10%
Volleyball		90%	10%	-
Wrestling		90%	10%	-

Table 5.1

There should be sufficient examples given here for you to be able to assess the specific demands of your own sport or your own particular part in it, for example the position you play.

5.10 Broad Brush Treatment of General Principles of Training

Broad to Specific
Start with a wide variety of training to improve the overall condition of your body in all respects. This is the base upon which you will build your fitness. Gradually make your training more and more specific to the activity in which you ultimately intend to perform. This thread of specificity should run right throughout your training from beginning to end. But towards the end your training should be almost totally specific. It is commonplace in many sports to repeat this broad to specific cycle each year starting in the off-season with the broad conditioning. Take care when doing this not to "play too hard" at first at activities you may not have done for a year, lest you injure yourself in the process.

There is often a period of a couple of months between selection for a national team and competition at the world championships. Athletes have to peak for the selection competition but they have to peak again for the world championships. It is a good idea between selection and final competition to do a bit of revision as you would for exams. Start again with broad, general training and cram a mini-season into the period between selection and competition, reaching a new peak for the big event

Train Individual Parts

Most sports demand not just one but a variety of talents and skills and place demands on more than one energy system and more than one muscle group. One way to increase the intensity of the training load and hence ultimately the training effect is to take one muscle group at a time or one energy system at a time and to train it separately. This can be done by devoting one complete training session, or part of each training session or a given period during the year to just one aspect. You should do this with each aspect, laying emphasis according either to your own weakest link or to the demands of your sport. Gradually you piece your individual parts of your overall fitness together, concluding as before, with the specific activity itself.

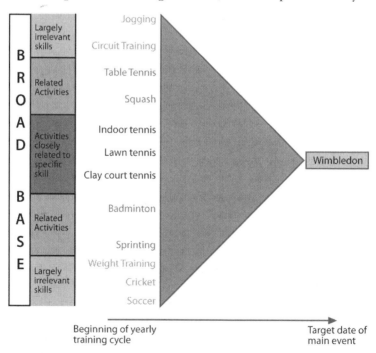

Figure 5.1

DIVIDING UP THE ACTIVITY
and training the individual parts

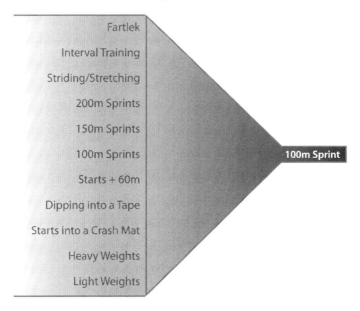

Figure 5.2

You can break any sport down into trainable bits like this. Do it for yours now. First take a broad brush dividing it into six or 10 parts. Then see how small those individual parts can be divided before you find it is impossible to break them down any further. You will be amazed at how much you will find that is trainable.

Creative Overloading

Again, no matter what sport you do, you can, by creative thinking, establish ways of overloading yourself. Just take the very simple example of throwing a javelin. By throwing a heavier javelin you can present your muscles with a greater load than normal. Inevitably the javelin will not go as far as normal which means that you will not be throwing it as fast as normal so in this respect, i.e. speed, your training using a heavy javelin will not be specific. However, by throwing a lighter javelin than normal you should be able to throw it further or at least faster. Here you will be overloading your muscles in terms of the speed with which they contract. You must however place the greatest emphasis on the specific activity of throwing the proper javelin, especially as you approach the competition season.

As a swimmer, you can increase the load on your arm and chest muscles by not using your legs, by holding paddles in your hands or having webbing between your fingers, by towing a bucket or simply by swimming faster for a shorter period. Provided that you allow time for recovery, you can do enough training at this faster speed, by repeating your sprints, to have a substantial strength training effect. I will go into this in more detail in the section on interval training. At the other end of the scale you can endure much longer periods of swimming by reducing the load on the arms with the aid of flippers on the feet. In this way you can do endurance training at a reduced load yet with the same speed of arm movement as you would normally have in your competitive situation. So although the load is reduced, the speed remains specific but the endurance (time the activity can be maintained at specific speed) is increased. Alternatively you can swim normally for longer than you would race so as to stress your endurance ability. But then you have to swim slower so speed would no longer be specific.

Inevitably in picking out one particular aspect to overload in some way, be it strength, speed, endurance or anaerobic glycolysis there is always some trade-off in specificity. It is important always to keep returning to activities that closely resemble the final competitive situation.

Specificity of Training
Specificity is all about doing in your training what you will actually be doing in your competition. In other words it is not so good improving the capacity of your oxygen uptake system by running if what you are ultimately aiming for is a swimming competition. You should be doing swimming training. This is a fairly obvious example but I will now quote less obvious ones.

Press-ups stress the pectoral muscles across the chest and the triceps muscles, which straighten the arms in a dynamic (moving) fashion. Also, there has to be an isometric contraction of the muscles of the trunk and back to keep the body straight. Isometric means one length or without changing length. So, in isometric muscle contractions, muscles do not change length, they merely develop tension. Press-ups are quite a strenuous exercise and many women cannot do them at all. It is commonplace for untrained men to be unable to do more than 15 and even amongst trained athletes it is not an exercise that can be performed aerobically, like running, for hours at a time. In other words, in its normal form, performed on a horizontal surface, it is an exercise limited by strength and as such it will train strength, the strength of the muscles I mentioned earlier. Yet it is an exercise to be found in almost every circuit training session designed to improve the aerobic capacity. If you want to train the oxygen system by circuit training then strength should not be the limiting factor in the performance of an exercise and so in the case of the press up it should be performed:

- on an incline
- with the feet on the ground and hands resting on a bench
- against a wall bar
- kneeling to reduce the weight that has to be lifted (a very full flexion is best as you then rest on the soft tissue of your lower thigh muscles rather than on the kneecap which can be quite painful)
- or it could be replaced with a bench press using a suitably lightly loaded barbell.

Having said all that, there are many sports in which the press up is a totally irrelevant exercise and it is a waste of time including it in a circuit in preparation for that sport. Take rowing for example. The only time during the rowing stroke that the hands push away from the body, as in a press up, is after the end of each stroke when the oar is out of the water and there is virtually no load on the pectorals or the triceps. A far more useful exercise for rowers would be the horizontal pull up, or bench pulls, precisely the reverse of the press up.

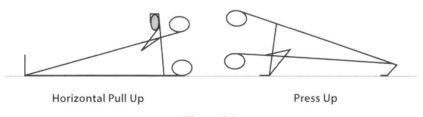

Horizontal Pull Up   Press Up

Figure 5.3

A point of further specificity here for rowers would be that in the pull up the hands should be held over-grasping the beam or bar rather than under-grasping it because in rowing they are rested on top of the oar not underneath. There is a variant of rowing called pulling (used in whalers, gigs and other substantial craft) where one hand is held under-grasp and the other over-grasp. Specificity in training should take the grasp into account and the pullers should do their horizontal rowing according to which side of the boat they row on. It might be better to alternate rather than building up an asymmetrical strength in the body. I try to discourage an imbalance in the strength of muscles from one side of the body to the other so as to reduce the risk of injury, especially to the back.

It has been established experimentally that the weight that athletes can push up using a two-leg press is less than the sum of the two individual single leg presses that the same athletes can lift. The exception to this finding is that rowers can, in fact, using both legs together (as in rowing) lift more than twice as much as they can lift with each leg singly. The implication for the training of rowers is that they should include in their training as much two-legged activity as possible. Jumping exercises would therefore be preferable to stepping exercises. Things like squat thrusts, squat jumps, squats, astride jumps, leg presses, cleans, snatches, tuck jumps, sit ups, double leg extensions and burpees all use both legs together and are to be preferred to high knee lifting, step ups, running on the spot, lunging etc. Having said this, variety is the spice of life and the extra load placed upon a single leg when bearing the whole weight is a legitimate and beneficial overload technique.

Fox, MacKenzie and Cohen trained some students on a cycle ergometer for a number of weeks. Some of them trained by cycling with their arms only and some with the legs only. The aerobic capacity of all of them improved over the training period whether cycling with the trained or untrained limbs. However, the investigators found that the improvement was substantially greater when the students were tested using the trained limbs than with the untrained limbs. This shows that although there were physiological changes taking place in the heart and lungs so as to improve the oxygen transport system, most of the physiological changes took place in the muscles themselves or were stimulated by the use of the muscles.

In another experiment by Stromme, Ingjer and Meen it was found that the maximum oxygen uptake of rowers, cyclists and skiers was higher in their specific sports activity than it was when running on a treadmill. This again demonstrates the need for specificity of training.

Even taking a group of non-athletic men, as Bouchard et al did, the same individual will have a different maximal aerobic power (max VO_2) when undertaking different activities, it being poorest in arm cranking and greatest in walking uphill on a motor driven treadmill.

The effects of training are so specific that it has been shown that a rower trained for double sculling had a significantly lower heart rate for any given level of work, as measured by his oxygen uptake (VO_2), when he was double sculling than when he was cycling or single sculling. In other words he was so in tune with the rhythm and stresses of double sculling that his body considered both cycling and single sculling to be equally unfamiliar and stressful despite the fact that single sculling is plainly much more akin to double sculling than cycling is. So you virtually cannot take the specificity of your training too far. If you are going to canoe K2 to then you should train in a K2. If you are going to row in an 8 then you should train in an 8. If you are to compete on a tandem then you should train on a tandem.

A lot of the specificity of the training result has to do with relaxed technique. If the movements required are in the least bit unfamiliar then untrained muscles will be brought into play to try to control the movements. As I mentioned earlier the use of untrained muscle groups results in impaired performance, be it in terms of strength, speed, anaerobic glycolysis, endurance or simply co-ordination.

The conclusion has to be that, for the competitive athlete, the training, which should be built upon a broad conditioning base, has ultimately to be totally specific down to the finest detail. This includes even training, as competition nears, at the exact race pace that you feel you will be capable of on the day, provided racing is involved in your sport. Clearly though, that ultimate race pace may only be sustainable for the full distance under race conditions when motivation is extremely high. So in training the inevitable trade-off in specificity means that you would have to practice that race pace for less than the race distance (see Tempo Training).

6 FROM STRENGTH TO STRENGTH

6.1 Danger

WARNING! Training can damage your health. Strength training often involves considerable strain. You know the sort of thing, red face, puffed out cheeks, yelling and shouting, blood vessels apparently about to pop out of your head or neck.

Very high blood pressures are created in this sort of situation and the heart muscle is under considerable strain. So if you have never done any training before, DON'T START HERE! First go back to the Chapter 3, DANGER OF DEATH, which is all about conditioning. If you are in any doubt go and have a medical check up first and tell your doctor what you are intending to do. This is especially important if you have a heart condition already, if you are overweight or if you have a family history of heart complaints.

Nevertheless strength training when properly controlled will induce beneficial changes in the heart.

6.2 Specificity

Needless to say you will not acquire strong legs by exercising your arms but specificity in strength training goes much further than this. By the end of this chapter you should know what to do to improve that specific aspect of strength that is required for your sport. First of all let me explain a little about muscle contractions and muscle types.

6.3 Types of Muscle Contraction

Isometric

This is the simplest form of contraction. Isometric means single length. The muscle does not change its length so no movement of limbs takes place and tension merely develops in the muscle. Arm wrestling across a table against an equal opponent gives rise to isometric muscle contractions. Such contractions are rare in sport but you will find them (or close approximations to isometric contractions) in climbing for example, gymnastics, shooting, rugby (in a stationary scrum), horse riding (particularly dressage) and trampolining and diving (when holding tension in the body) to name but a few. Often isometric contractions will be taking place in some muscles (to hold part of the body firm) while dynamic contractions are taking place in other muscles.

Isokinetic

In isokinetic contractions the limb being acted upon by the muscle moves at a constant speed. Again such contractions are rare in sport being found mainly in sports where a fluid provides the resistance so that a small increase in speed produces a considerable increase in resistance and the inclination is therefore to maintain a constant speed. Examples are sports where this occurs are swimming, rowing, canoeing and cycling.

Dynamic

These are contractions in which movement occurs, not necessarily at constant speed, nor necessarily against constant load. They are sometimes incorrectly referred to as isotonic meaning that a constant tension is maintained throughout the contraction.

Isotonic

This is nearly impossible to achieve and almost certainly does not occur when lifting a constant load against gravity because of two factors. Firstly, the muscle acts by lever action on the bones and the tension required to support the load changes as the joint angle changes. Secondly, load has inertia, which means that the load would like to carry on moving uniformly or remain stationary unless acted upon by another force. So once you have got a load moving (horizontally) you can maintain its velocity with a reduced force. Alternatively, you can accelerate it more with a greater force. Exactly what tension is being developed in a muscle is difficult to establish with a moving load, but it is not impossible and a constant muscle tension is very rare.

Dynamic contractions fall into two further categories, concentric and eccentric, which were mentioned in the chapter on conditioning.

Concentric

If the muscle shortens during a dynamic contraction then this is known as a concentric (towards the centre) contraction.

Eccentric

If the muscle is lengthened during a dynamic contraction then this is known as an eccentric contraction. Remember that eccentric contractions give rise to greater delayed muscular soreness than do concentric contractions. Dynamic contractions are the most common in sports and eccentric contractions are usually used to advantage in many activities because greater tension can be developed in the muscle this way.

6.4 Training Effects Specific to Contraction Type

Isometric training, not surprisingly, gives rise to improvements in isometric strength. What is surprising is that the strength is specific to the angle of the joint at which the training takes place. So training the muscle isometricly in one small range of the muscle length will give rise to an increase in isometric strength at that length. The improvements in strength at other lengths will not be so significant.

Isokinetic training improves isokinetic strength. The gain in strength though is greatest at or below the speed of contraction used in training. This is a good reason for including in your training, movements that are quicker than you will ultimately use in competition. There is a tendency to increase the load in the hope of gaining an improvement in strength without having regard to the fact that the increased load reduces the speed at which the movement may be executed. The speed of contraction is as important as the tension developed in the contraction. DO NOT FORGET THIS.

Dynamic training against a constant load has the disadvantage that the muscle only develops maximum tension at one point in the range of movement. This is because of the lever action mentioned earlier. Sometimes the load itself changes during a muscle contraction and again there is usually a peak load at some point in the contraction. At all other points the muscle is at a submaximal tension and the training effect is not as great. When you are using weights to provide a progressive overload it is important to bear this in mind and try to approach as closely as possible the exact movement that you will perform in competition with the peak load occurring at the same point.

6.5 Injury Risk

It has been my unfortunate experience to observe that very few athletes injure themselves in competition and that the majority of those who do get injured do so during training. I refer you back to the chapter on conditioning yet again, Chapter 3 DANGER OF DEATH. If you are going to be doing maximal muscle contractions then you must first condition yourself for them.

6.6 The Genetic Endowment

We are all born with certain numbers of muscle fibres and that cannot be changed. We also have a certain mix of fibre types. Some have more of one type than another type and some are the other way around. This cannot be changed either. However, we can adapt what we are born with to the task by training and although we may never be able to achieve what a more gifted athlete can achieve, nevertheless we can improve by training.

6.7 Muscle Fibre Types

There are two basic types of muscle fibre, commonly known as slow twitch or Type I and fast twitch or Type II.

Type I

Slow twitch fibres have a slow contraction speed, hence their name. They are associated with endurance activity and have all the necessary requirements to fulfil this role. They have high myoglobin content (that stores oxygen), a high enzyme activity in the mitochondria (useful for aerobic metabolism) and they have a high density of blood capillaries (for supplying the tissue with blood and oxygen). Endurance athletes have a greater cross-sectional area of these Type I fibres than normal. This does not mean that they are necessarily born with more of these slow-twitch fibres than the rest of us but if they are they have a clear advantage. In endurance activities these fibres are preferentially selected, rather than the fast twitch fibres, and endurance training therefore affects these fibres first and foremost.

Type II

Fast twitch fibres have, surprise, surprise, a high contraction speed. They are preferentially recruited by the central nervous system to contract where great speed and force are required. They are endowed with a plentiful supply of the enzymes needed for the phosphagen energy liberation system and also for anaerobic glycolysis, that energy system responsible for the production of lactic acid. Unlike the Type I fibres their mitochondrial enzyme activity is low and their myoglobin content and capillary density are low, so consequently they have poor endurance. The difference in blood supply between the fibre types leads to some difference in colour. The Type I muscle tissue being more red and the Type II more white.

Sub-types

The fast twitch fibres can be further subdivided into Type IIa and Type IIb. There is a third type but this is not common in humans. The Type IIa tend not to have quite so good a glycolytic capacity as the Type IIb but they do have a greater the aerobic potential. This makes them more adaptive and that together with an increase in capillarization due to training can virtually convert them into supplementary Type I fibres. As fast twitch fibres are preferentially recruited for strength based activities it follows that if you are genetically endowed with more of them than normal then your response to strength training will be better than normal.

6.8 Training Methods

Well that is enough theory for now. What you want to know is how to improve your strength. You should have realised by now that it is very important that you know what it is you want your muscles to do because this is what you must train them for. Before you press on, just stop a moment and think about your sport.

You do not need to know all the Latin names of all the muscles you use in your sport. You only have to be able to work out which muscles are used in which way in your sport. Go through the actions you would typically expect to perform, no matter how varied they may be and work out for each muscle group what type of muscle contractions you perform and whether the activity is a fast twitch, strength oriented one or a slow twitch, endurance type of activity. When you have done this you can start to develop a training programme based on specificity.

If you simply want your muscles to get bigger, as you might if you were a body builder, then your objective must be to exercise them maximally in the full range of movement. If, on the other hand, you want your muscles to do a job like putting the shot or jumping over a bar then you have to be much more particular about the way that you train them.

6.9 How to Overload Muscles

To understand how to overload muscles you need to understand that a muscle group is made up of many thousands of smaller parts and that these are brought into play on an ALL OR NOTHING basis. So to create greater tension in a muscle group requires that a greater number of muscle fibres be used. To create maximal tension all the muscle fibres must work together. This is a very rare occurrence. The nervous system inhibits the contraction of the total muscle group and it is only in life or death situations or through hypnotism or electric shock that complete tetanus, as it is known, is brought about. There is a case documented of a woman who lifted a car that had rolled onto her baby. She created such force in her muscles that she fused together vertebrae in her spine!

Training can disinhibit the central nervous system allowing the recruitment of more and more muscle fibres. It does not appear that you have to do your absolute maximum in order to have a training effect. Because each muscle fibre is contracting maximally in its own way, each muscle fibre will be subject to a training effect, and over time more and more contractile protein will be laid down in each muscle fibre so that it actually grows. This is known as hypertrophy. However, if you do not subject muscles to a progressive increase in stress, they will eventually conclude that they are strong enough for the job you are asking them to do and will not adapt anymore. You must, by progressively increasing the load on your muscles, persuade the central nervous system to recruit more and more fibres to do the job if strength is what you require.

As there are four types of muscle contraction, isometric, isokinetic, concentric and eccentric there are four similar types of training for muscular strength. The concentric and eccentric training is combined in dynamic weight training or training against spring loads, for example. However, particular emphasis can be placed upon the concentric contractions by letting go of loads after the concentric contraction thereby avoiding the eccentric contractions, which you will remember give rise to greater delayed muscular soreness.

6.10 Isometric Training

Maximal or near maximal isometric contractions held for about five seconds and repeated as few as five to ten times each day for five days each week will produce strength gains. Depending on how highly trained you are already these gains can be of the order of five percent per week.

This sounds too easy to be true, doesn't it? Isometrics do have the advantage of taking up a very small proportion of your time. They also require virtually no equipment as muscles can be tensed isometricly one against another, flexor against extensor. The sort of stretching that you do when you wake-up is a typical, naturally occurring form of isometric contraction and you can build on these natural movements to create quite a strenuous isometric programme. If I give you examples, it may restrict your creativity. Go-ahead, try it.

Because they do not require any equipment the exercises, which you can invent yourself to exercise the muscles you want, can be done in a small space, sitting in a car in a traffic jam for example. Wild cats kept in cages in zoos use isometrics to maintain their strength and it was this observation that led Charles Atlas to develop his "Dynamic Tension" method of body building early in the 20th century. Because isometric contractions only develop strength at the joint angle at which the contraction takes place, the overall strength has to be achieved by varying the joint angle. In other words by performing contractions at different points in the whole range of movement. If the limb is moved during an isometric contraction it ceases to be an isometric contraction and becomes a slow dynamic movement. This is the principal, I assume, of Atlas's "Dynamic Tension" method. It is also used in an ancient Chinese movement form known as Tai Chi or shadow boxing. Take an early morning walk in China and you will discover hundreds of people, young and old but especially the old, performing these ritualised martial arts movements.

Just try it for yourself in front of a mirror. After a few minutes of slow, deliberate movements maintaining as much tension in your body as possible you will be quite exhausted. This is partly because the tension creation is work that consumes energy and partly because the tension constricts blood flow leading to a higher blood pressure and raised heart rate.

Isometric contractions, by the creation of the high blood pressure, will have a training effect on the heart, whose muscular walls will thicken eventually and also enjoy greater capillarization. However there is a danger for the post-coronary patient. My own belief is that prevention of injury by proper conditioning is quite preferable to cure and that this applies as much to heart muscle has to any other organ in the body. So whilst you are healthy a progressive isometric training programme to build up the strength of your heart muscle wall cannot do any harm.

6.11 Isokinetic Training

This form of training is considered to be very safe on the whole. One typical form of isokinetic training much used in rehabilitation and therapy is swimming. The contractions are really only safe as long as reasonable speeds of movement are possible. At slower speeds much greater force is developed in the muscles and the same reservations that apply to isometric contractions and the lifting of heavyweights must be held.

Most isokinetic programmes involve the use of machines that fall into one of two categories. Either they contain governors to regulate the speed of rotation of some device that is set spinning by the muscles action or else they have hydraulic or pneumatic devices which tend to compress at one particular speed no matter how much force is used to compress them, within reason. Either way the muscles find that they can develop maximal tension throughout the whole range of movement that the machine demands. Rowing machines are almost isokinetic and the best ones do a good job of simulating the feeling of rowing, apart from the obvious shortcomings, like scenery whizzing by! Rowing itself is not quite isokinetic as speed does change during the stroke, inevitably, especially in small light boats.

The exactly constant speed muscle contraction is rare in sport because most movements in sport require acceleration in order to achieve as high a final speed as possible. Sometimes the time available to achieve this acceleration is small; such as in the time a runner's foot is in contact with the ground. In cycling the pedals move around at a constant angular velocity but this does not mean that the angular velocity of the limbs driving the pedals is constant. Cycling, however, does provide the cyclist with the opportunity to work his muscles at maximal tension throughout the range of their movement, which is the object of isokinetic training. Anybody who has done bi- or triathlons will know, however, that it is useless to use cycling as training for running or swimming. So we are back to specificity.

Isokinetic programs do enable the muscles to be loaded maximally throughout the range of the movement of the machine upon which the work is being done. However, if the movement required or permitted by the machine is not similar to the movement required by your sport it is pretty fruitless training on it. Conversely if the movement required by the machine is closely allied to your sport's activity, such as in the best sports simulators, then it is ideal as a training activity. This is especially so at times of the year when it is impossible to do your main sport e.g. when rivers and roads are frozen in winter.

Training on isokinetic machines can be geared towards strength or endurance or the lactic acid system. To train for strength the load has to be great enough so that only a few repetitions of the movement can be performed. The optimum number, based on experience of dynamic training regimes, would probably be six repetitions but I am not aware of any experiments that have been conducted to prove this. If you are able to do many hundreds of repetitions then you are not training strength. If after a minute or so you find that you have to stop because of a burning pain in your muscles then you are using the lactic acid system. Strength training and speed training should be conducted in short maximal bursts with plenty of rest in between. The effort should not last for more than 30 seconds at a time and would more usually be confined to less than 15 seconds.

Remember that isokinetic training is speed specific and the greatest training effect is **at** or **below** the training speed with small improvements above the training speed.

6.12 Eccentric Training

In eccentric training the emphasis is placed upon eccentric muscle contractions where the muscle is lengthened by a load that exceeds the tension that the muscle is producing. Coaches have been fairly dismissive of this method of training in the past, probably for two reasons. Firstly, the severe delayed muscle soreness caused by eccentric contractions. This type of soreness is quite different from the acute soreness experienced during maximal contractions which is largely due to waste products such as potassium and lactic acid building up in the muscle because of the impaired blood flow during the contraction. Delayed muscle soreness on the other hand leaves the muscle feeling more tender to the touch and also weaker. It is this weakness that follows eccentric training that is the second reason why coaches have ignored it as a valid form of training in the past. Certainly the weakness experienced is a very good reason for avoiding eccentric contractions if at all possible during the week before a competition in which no eccentric contractions are required. There are, of course, many sports where eccentric contractions are commonplace and cannot be avoided. In these sports where the athlete is familiar with the eccentric contractions used there appears to be no harm in using them in training.

One of the main features of the muscle tension that can be attained within any particular group is that it varies according to the length of the muscle. The maximum tension that a muscle can produce occurs when it is 20 percent longer than its equilibrium length. The equilibrium length is the length the muscle would be if it were relaxed and not attached to anything at either end. Interestingly most muscles when resting are stretched to the optimum length for producing maximum tension i.e. 1.2 times the equilibrium length and if you were to snip the tendons at each end the muscle would shorten to its equilibrium length merely because of its own natural elasticity. If the muscle is stretched beyond its optimum length the tension it is capable of producing diminishes. Similarly, as the muscle shortens below the optimum length, again its ability to create tension reduces, falling to zero eventually at around 60 percent of its equilibrium length.

A more interesting feature of the tension a muscle is able to create, which has particular application to eccentric training, is the relation of this tension to the speed of the contraction. As you might expect, during a concentric contraction the tension falls off as the speed of contraction increases till eventually the muscle can only create enough force to shorten itself. The application of any load would slow the muscle contraction down.

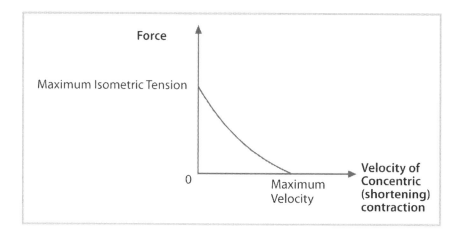

Figure 6.1

If the force/velocity curve were similar for eccentric contractions, then an increase in the load on the muscle beyond the maximum isometric tension would mean a sudden and catastrophic lengthening of the muscle.

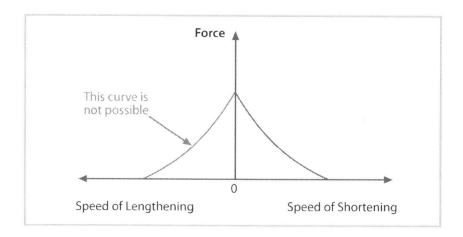

Figure 6.2

Instead, the tension in the muscle continues to increase as heavier loads are applied to it and the velocity of lengthening increases also. Eventually a point is reached where a small increase in load on the muscle gives rise to a substantial increase in the speed of lengthening.

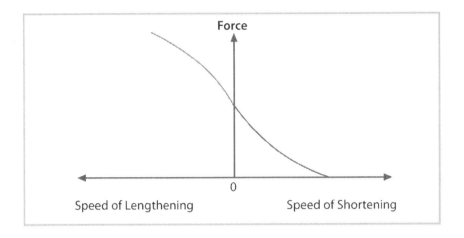

Figure 6.3

This means that a greater tension can be developed in the muscle when it is lengthening during an eccentric contraction than can be developed isometricly or concentrically. It follows that eccentric training is an intensive form of training and that it can therefore be used in the development of strength. There is no evidence however, to indicate any advantage in strength gain using eccentric programs to the strength gain using isometric or concentric programs. The disadvantages outlined earlier, however, are clear enough.

Plyometrics
This is a form of eccentric/concentric training that really makes use of the muscle spindle or myotatic reflex and the stored energy in the stretch of a tensed muscle. It consists mainly of jumping, bounding and hopping exercises to train the legs but a variation long used in the training of the triceps in gymnastics is the pump swing on the parallel bars. The idea is that a concentric contraction has long been known to be stronger if immediately preceded by optimum eccentric contraction. The clearest example of this is the extra height that can be attained in a standing jump if immediately preceded by a squatting movement as opposed to starting already squatting, say seated on a chair. In the former case, where a rebound effect takes place, tension is developing in the muscles of the legs whilst they are still being stretched and considerable tension already exists in the muscles at the point of change of direction. In this way a greater total accelerating force can be generated whilst the feet are in contact with the ground.

How much of the extra power is due to the action of the myotatic reflex and how much is due to stored energy in the elastic stretch of the muscle is not known but the phenomenon is used extensively in sports, often without people realising they are using it.

The Russians have made Plyometric training popular. Borzov the double gold medallist in 100 and 200m in 1972 used it as part of his training and many well-known Western athletes since have used it. Most of the plyometric techniques involve the use of boxes or benches of varying heights. You can jump off one, say 18 inches (450 mm) high and when you land on the ground you execute a rebound jump straight away, perhaps onto another box. The jumps can involve twists and can be one legged or two legged so that they can be made more specific to the sport or event for which you are training.

A shot putter for example might start his putting action by jumping backwards off a six inch high box into the middle of the putting circle. This would specifically over load the putting/driving leg. A rower would be best to jump backwards off one box to the ground and back onto another with a fairly deep knee bend and hip flexion during the ground landing so as to approach, as closely as possible, the rowing situation. A high jumper could jump onto a 6-inch to 12-inch box on the penultimate step of a 3-5 step run up. The last step would be down onto the ground level again before performing the jump. Boxes could be placed as obstacles for a triple jumper to hop or step over. Or they could be used to provide extra height so that in a landing for take-off the plyometric aspect of jumping is emphasised and the active leg is overloaded.

The changes that can be rung using the plyometric techniques are limited only by your imagination. However, when you are developing plyometric exercises for your specific activity, remember that you will need conditioning to them if they are new to you so you don't overdo it. Remember that a plyometrics session is intensive and is aimed at quality, speed, power, strength, height or length. This means that you should be fresh when you do plyometrics and that you should warm up first and you will need to recover afterwards. As they emphasise eccentric contractions you should avoid them two weeks prior to any major event.

Sessions can start at one per week building up to 4 per week if necessary with intensity increasing from 25 to 220 "contacts" per session. These would normally be split up into groups of jumps with repetitions varying from 2 contacts to 20 contacts per exercise. I will go into typical ways these could be programmed when I come to the design of training programs.

Personally I think that there is a grave danger of stumbling and injuring yourself in plyometrics. This rather defeats their purpose. So beware!

6.13 Concentric/Dynamic Training

This sort of training is generally performed with free weights, barbells and dumbbells but weights can be confined to move in a particular path in such training machines as the leg press or pec dec. The difference with free weights is that peripheral muscles are brought into use during lifts in order to control accurately the direction of movement and to maintain good balance. With a machine the direction of movement is determined by the machine and balance is not critical. They are usually much safer than free weights, however, and by clever design with the use of levers, pulleys and cams they can be made to stress muscles in ways that free weights cannot.

Springs can also be used for dynamic strength training. The extension of the spring obeys Hooke's law insofar as it is proportional directly to the load applied. The harder you pull on a spring the more it stretches. This means that the strength required to extend the spring increases as the extension increases.

Let us compare leg pressing of a weight and leg pressing of a spring.

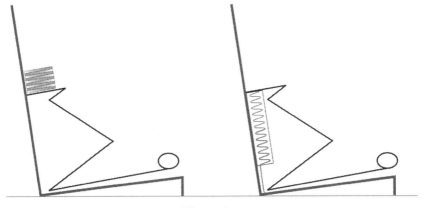

Figure 6.4

In the case of the weights you will find that if you take the load onto your feet with your legs straight it is easy to support a massive load. However, the more you bend your legs the greater is the difficulty you will have in supporting it. If the load is too great then you will reach a point where your legs would give way, which is why leg press machines are provided with stops to prevent you from being stuck under the weights or badly injured by them.

The reason the weight feels heavier the lower it gets is simply that the load is further away from the knee joint and so the leg muscles have to produce more torque in order to overcome the load presented by the weight. (Torque is the same as moment and is the rotational equivalent of force, which is a linear vector). Skip the following technical explanation if you wish.

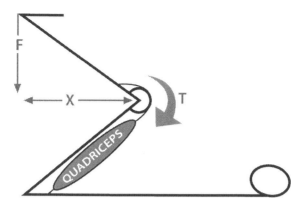

Figure 6.5

The load produces an anti-clockwise moment about the knee joint of F.x that has to be overcome by the clockwise moment T at the knee provided by the quadriceps muscle group. The smaller x is, the lower T can be until when x is zero no anti-clockwise torque exists and so no clockwise torque is needed to overcome it. Consequently supporting a heavy weight with straight legs is relatively effortless.

Conversely when the knee joint is fully flexed and x is therefore large the anti-clockwise torque F.x is large and the clockwise torque T needed to overcome it is also large. (To simplify the explanation, a similar story about what happens at the hip joint has been ignored and it has been assumed that the weight is pushed up vertically).

The repercussions of this for leg pressing are that the muscles will be maximally loaded *only* in the fully flexed position if weights are used to provide the resistance. The same applies for the squat exercise.

However, if a spring is used the force F needed to overcome the tension in the spring is proportional to the extension of the spring so that as x gets shorter when the knees straighten the force F gets larger.

When the legs are straight the torque required to overcome Fx is still zero because x is zero. When the legs are bent, provided there is no extension of the spring F is zero so Fx is again zero and the torque T can be zero. This is quite different to the weights situation where the torque T is zero when the legs are straight and increases to a maximum when the legs are bent. With a spring the torque developed at the knee is zero when the legs are both bent and straight with the maximum torque occurring at some point in between. If the maximum torque T is large enough to overcome the maximum load provided by the spring then it will be possible to extend the legs fully. If T cannot exceed Fx then a point will be reached where the legs cannot be further extended and you will be considered to have failed in the lift.

So here we have two methods of training the leg extensor muscles that are quite different. In one, with the weights, the maximum tension has to be developed with the legs fully bent. In the other, maximum tension can be developed at any point up to about half way, depending upon the stiffness of the spring. However, if you can get past the halfway point you will be able to perform a full leg extension without maximal tension in the latter part of the leg extension. Exactly where the theoretical point of maximum torque development should be is a relatively easy mathematical calculation but it is not important to know. What *is* important to understand is the difference between spring action and the action of weights under the attraction of gravity. Both have their place in the development of strength and are equally valid if sufficient load is used.

The isokinetic machines I mentioned earlier, of course, enable you to perform leg extensions with maximal tension in the muscles throughout the whole movement. This is obviously of great benefit if you desire the muscles to develop strength throughout their range but remember that the demands of specificity in training means that such full range strength may be superfluous in your particular sport.

Body builders, of course, do try to develop all their muscles maximally and in all ranges of movement in order to leave no stone unturned, as it were, in their quest for bigger and better muscles. If this is what you require then a variety of machines and lifts working on the same muscle groups in different ways will be useful to you. Isokinetic machines have their place but with many of the cheaper ones there is no means of measuring the tension, torque or power developed so there is no means of assessing your progress as your strength develops. The better machines are provided with such devices.

There is an alternative way of using weights working against gravity that will produce a maximal torque and therefore maximal tension in muscles throughout the whole range of movement and this is by the use of cams, pulleys and levers. Nautilus have gone into this method in a big way and produce a wide variety of machines of a sturdy construction which enable you to perform graduated workouts and to assess your progress easily because the loads can be varied by changing the weights.

There is a clear advantage in the use of Nautilus equipment over free weights insofar as injuries are concerned. One United States university in the knowledge that it was going to acquire Nautilus equipment conducted a survey of sport injuries amongst students before and after the equipment was installed. The result was a staggering two-thirds reduction in the number of injuries!

6.14 Repetition Maxima

Most weight training programmes are based upon the idea of performing several sets of repetitions of a particular exercise at various percentages of your maximum ability. Your maximum ability can be defined in many ways but the idea of a 10 repetition maximum or a 6-repetition maximum or a 3 repetition maximum etc. is an easy one to latch onto. It means the maximum weight that you can lift, with good technique, i.e. safely, 10, 6 or 3 times. Usually your 3-repetition maximum is going to be a higher figure than your 10 repetition maximum. The terms are abbreviated to 10RM, 6RM, and 3RM. Your 1RM is the maximum weight that you can lift once but this is not used as a basis for calculation of your training loads.

One of the earliest dynamic, progressive, resistance-training programmes was advocated by Delorme and Watkins in 1948 and is still used effectively by many athletes and body builders today. It involves three sets of 10 repetitions each.

(Warm up) Set 1 = 10 reps with load of 50% of 10RM
Set 2 = 10 reps with load of 75% of 10RM
Set 3 = 10 reps with load of 100% of 10RM.

Each set of repetitions must be performed without rest between the repetitions. When more than 10 repetitions can be performed with the 10RM load then be load should be increased so that the muscles are always being progressively overloaded.

The variations on this basic theme, of course, are considerable. From studies undertaken by Berger it appears that, from a variety of combinations tried, using different numbers of sets and repetitions three sets of 6RM came out top. This involved 18 repetitions altogether of 100% of the 6RM load so clearly a substantial rest between each set would be required.

6.15 Circuit Training

One way of doing this without wasting too much time standing around resting is to perform your exercises in a circuit. Obviously the exercises would need to be chosen carefully so that the same muscle group is not taxed two or three times in quick succession. If you do this you will not be training strength, you will be training endurance. Whilst training the endurance of your muscles is a perfectly legitimate activity it is not the objective here. Many people make the mistake, in designing their circuits, of forgetting what it is they are training. If you are training strength or speed then adequate rest is essential for the full recovery of the muscles. This rest should be *at least* three times the duration of the exercise set itself so this lends itself to training in small groups. If you make the mistake of putting together exercises that are too similar then the load that can be lifted will have to be lower and the emphasis will be on quantity instead of quality.

6.16 *Typical Strength Circuit*

Exercise	Main Muscle Groups Used
Military press behind the neck	Triceps, deltoids, trapezius
Squats	Quadriceps, gluteus maximus
Curls	Biceps, brachioradialis
Pec Dec	Pectorals
Sit ups with weight	Rectus abdominis, quadriceps
Bench pull (horizontal rowing)	Biceps, brachioradialis, latissimus dorsi
Dead lift	Quadriceps, gluteus maximus, dorsals, erectors, trapezius, rectus abdominis
Bench press	Triceps, pectorals
Pull ups	Biceps, latissimus dorsi

Many body builders will pick just two muscle groups per day to train, a large one such as the upper legs or trunk and a small one such as the triceps, deltoids or calf muscles. They will use a variety of exercises aimed at the same muscle group exercising it in different ranges of movement. The number of repetitions using this method of training takes us into the realm of muscular endurance and the training effect is upon such things as vascularization of the muscle, i.e. increasing the number of blood vessels in the muscle. This gives the bodybuilder the facility to pump up the muscles with blood for competitions.

The reason they pick only two muscle groups per day is so that they can train everyday. Using weights or springs you will find that almost every concentric muscle contraction is either preceded or succeeded by an eccentric contraction. With so many eccentric contractions in a training session the muscles become very sore for several days and maximal contractions cannot be performed for four or five days. So by splitting the body up and training a bit each day bodybuilders are able to rest some muscle groups whilst training others.

As it is the fast twitch fibres that grow (hypertrophy) when subjected to strength training it does not seem to be too logical when attempting to increase muscle cross-sectional area to train using so many repetitions, say 100 for one muscle group in a training session. It would, in my view, be better to use an isokinetic machine or one of the Nautilus machines so that the full range of movement is fully taxed only a few times with good rests in between. This should have the most substantial effects on complete muscle strength and hence muscle size. If eccentric contractions are involved then adequate rest must be provided. If only concentric contractions are performed then training can take place more frequently.

6.17 Power

In strength training for most sports the maximum force that can be produced is not as important as the maximum power that can be produced. Power is rate of work. Work is force times distance moved in the direction of force. So power is also force times velocity.

$P = F.v$

Let us look at a simple weight lifting example. Suppose you lift a weight of 50 kg through height of 1.5m in 0.25 seconds then ignoring the work you have done in lifting your own body weight we can calculate your power output as follows. The force of gravity on the 50 kg weight is 50 times 9.81 Newtons where 9.81 m/s/s would be the acceleration, g, due to gravity.

Power = 50 x 9.81 x 1.5 / 0.25 watts
= 2,943 W
= 2.943 kW

Let us suppose that to perform six repetitions takes you five seconds

Power = 50 x 9.81 x 1.5 x 6 / 5
= 882.9 watts
= 0.88 kW

This is lower for two reasons. Firstly, in this case we are including in the time the repeated putting down of the weight, which was not included in the first example. Secondly, because you are doing the exercise six times I have assumed that you will be a bit slower overall than if you did it once.

Now this is where you can kid yourself that you are making progress when you are not really making useful progress at all. Suppose you find that you can increase your 6RM to 60kg but that in order to do so the time taken to perform it increases to seven seconds. What would your power output now be?

Power = 60 x 9.81 x 1.5 x 6 / 7
= 756 watts
= 0.76 kW

So although your 6RM has gone up by 20 percent your power (rate of work) has gone down.

It is important, therefore, in training for sports where power is a requirement to keep a check on the time it takes you to do your training sessions. It does not matter so much in training for speed and power if you find you require more rest between sets in order to maintain a high power output. But it does matter if you take more time to perform the work in each set. Remember that all training should be specific and specificity applies to speed as much as anything else.

6.18 Strength Retention

Fortunately the maintenance of strength is not so difficult as the acquisition of strength and as little as one repetition of your 1RM lift per week can be enough to retain and even improve upon the strength you have built up. This has repercussions for sports people who have competitive and non-competitive seasons. During the off-season strength can be built up. During the competitive season when, owing to the demands of competition, strength training is considered either undesirable or too time-consuming a strength retention programme can be undertaken instead. Consequently the benefits of the out of season strength training will not be lost.

6.19 Specificity and Conditioning

A final word again about specificity. Many sports movements are difficult to replicate in a gymnasium and you will have to be very ingenious to think of exercises that can be used to train progressively the exact muscles you use in your sport. This is an opportunity for you to be creative but remember that whenever you do anything even slightly new or different you will require a period of conditioning or you will risk injury.

6.20 Diet

Strenuous training produces bigger and stronger muscles but for them to grow you need the appropriate building materials, protein.

Some bodybuilders eat as many as 20 egg whites per day! MORE SIGNIFICANT THOUGH, and more often overlooked by strength trainers is that enormous amounts of energy are also required, mainly in the form of carbohydrates, which the body turns into glycogen, in order to do the training at the required intensity. Vast quantities of food of the right type are required when undertaking exceptionally arduous training and a considerable portion of the expense involved in participation in strength sports goes on food.

Without the proper food it is impossible to undertake the heavy training required at the top-level. In fact the ability to digest enough food is a limiting factor in the amount of quality training that top athletes can undertake. There simply isn't enough time in the day. Read more about diet in Chapter 10, FUEL SUPPLY LIMITATION.

7 EXPLOSIVE ATTACK

7.1 Training Energy Systems

As I already described to you in my submarine analogy the body has three main energy systems, the phosphagen system, the lactic acid system and the oxygen system. The phosphagen system can be split down further into the ATP system (the primary energy system which is ultimately responsible for all work done and without which we could not even lift a cup and saucer) and the PC system, which is the initial reserve for the ATP system. However, for the purpose of training, the ATP and PC systems can be considered one. The oxygen system uses either carbohydrate or fat as fuel and the rate of release of energy is greater from carbohydrate than from fat. However, the body's stores of energy in the form of fat are greater than its carbohydrate stores and in long duration exercise fat is used in increasing proportion. Carbohydrate is nevertheless necessary for the metabolism of fat and without any carbohydrate the body will almost grind to a halt. Anaerobic glycolysis, the breakdown of glycogen (carbohydrate) as a fuel in the absence of oxygen, is capable of a high rate of energy release, somewhere between the phosphagen system and the oxygen system but it unfortunately produces lactic acid as a by-product and this leads to fatigue.

The emphasis placed by the body on one energy source or another depends upon the duration of the exercise being undertaken, the intensity of the effort and whether the activity is continuous or intermittent. Once you know which energy systems your particular sport makes use of, and in which proportions, you can start to train them. In the next few chapters I will explain to you some more of the interplay amongst the energy systems, how they can be overloaded and progressively stressed and what happens during recovery from exercise. I will cover interval training, circuit training, continuous training, fartlek, alternate training, speed work, and tempo and over-distance training. Later I will show you how to design a training programme. You will then have all the necessary tools to get fit enough to win. But being fit will not be enough. Finally you have to learn HOW to WIN and that is what the chapter 14, Mind Your Head, is about.

7.2 Training the Phosphagen System

You need the phosphagen system for sprinting and for explosive movements of short duration. If the energy stores in the form of ATP and PC are inadequate for the task set then anaerobic glycolysis will have to take place so that you can continue at all. However, you will not be able to go as fast and lactic acid will eventually bring you to a halt. Clearly it would be of benefit if the ATP and PC stores could be increased so that the whole task could be performed as fast as possible and without recourse to anaerobic glycolysis. Also, if you have to perform intermittent sprinting, as in most ball games, then it would be useful if the body's ability to replenish the stores quickly could be improved.

7.3 Sprint Interval Training

The best way to overload the phosphagen system is to deplete the ATP and PC stores repeatedly, allowing adequate time for replenishment so that the speed and quality of your movements can be maintained. You cannot simply extend the duration of an all out sprint in the hope of overloading the system. That simply will not work because you will no longer be stressing the phosphagen system, you will be using anaerobic glycolysis. You must simply stop working before any appreciable accumulation of lactic acid has taken place and then rest while the oxygen system goes to work providing the energy for re-building ATP molecules from ADP and phosphagen and also for rebuilding phosphocreatine, PC. Very light exercise, walking, flexing is acceptable during this period but the emphasis should be on rest. Complete recovery of the phosphagen stores takes at least two minutes and at most five minutes but it is not necessary to wait this long unless you are really going for all out quality of movement. You can progressively deplete the store by allowing insufficient time for recovery, say 30 seconds and then sprinting again. After say 10 repetitions of a 10-second work bout with 30 seconds rest between, a longer more complete rest would be required, say five minutes, before performing another set of repetitions. Probably five sets of 10 x 10-second work bouts would be sufficient for one training session.

The longer the work bouts the more likely you are to be using the lactic acid system. This would be beneficial if, as is often the case, your sport places demands on both systems. But for work bouts up to about 25 seconds, with rest relief in between each work bout lasting three times as long as the duration of the work, you will be overloading the ATP - PC system most of all.

TRAINING PRESCRIPTIONS FOR ATP - PC SYSTEM

Work Bout Duration (Sec)	Repetitions per Set	Sets per Training Session	Rest between Repetitions (Sec)	Rest between Sets (Min)
10	10	5	30	5
15	9	5	45	5
20	10	4	60	5
25	8	4	75	5

Table 7.1

7.4 Training Effect of Interval Sprints

Muscles

Following a training programme of this type the concentrations of ATP and PC in the muscles has been shown to increase along with increases in the concentrations of the enzymes responsible for the breakdown of phosphagens and also for their resynthesis. Of course, the effects are specific to the muscles used in the training so here is another reason to make the training you are doing resemble as closely as possible the ultimate activity in which you intend to compete.

Heart

As with strength training, much sprint training involves high levels of muscle tension with a consequent increase in blood pressure during exercise. This has the same strength training effect on the heart muscle, which thickens and strengthens as a result. I liken the strength-trained heart to a hot water bottle, which it is virtually impossible to burst when you blow into it. Of course, it does not expand very much either, so its capacity is not large. The endurance trained heart, on the other hand, I compare with a party balloon that can be blown up to a substantial size even though it is small to start with. Its walls are thin but its capacity is large. We call this capacity the stroke volume i.e. the volume of blood the heart can pump in one stroke and I will refer to this later in relation to the oxygen system.

Nervous System

Sprint training teaches you how to move fast. As a schoolboy I always used to struggle to go fast in my interval training over periods of one minute, 45 seconds and especially 30 seconds until a coach took me aside and suggested we do a series of 10 seconds sprints together. I had never done this before and the benefit was immediately apparent. I joined in with my usual training partners in their final 30-second sprint and for the first time ever I was able to keep up with them.

You see sprinting, in whatever sport, involves quite different movements to those involved in endurance or middle distance. The rhythm is different, balance is different, the time available for application of force or power is shorter, muscles have to contract faster which may involve the recruitment of more fast twitch fibres with a higher twitch threshold so muscle fibres that were not used before suddenly come into play. In other words, it is just like learning a new skill.

If you are ever going to develop a fast start or a sprint finish you must learn how to move fast and so sprint training is an essential element for the majority of sports. How big a part sprint training should play is determined by the table 5.1 in Chapter 5 OVERLOADED SUBMARINE which is all about Physical Training.

Heart Rate

During exercise of an explosive or sprint nature the heart rate will rise substantially to near the maximal level. Your maximum heart rate HR is approximately 220 - your age, so if you are 25 your maximum heart rate is likely to be approximately 195. This is a rule of thumb, not a hard and fast rule. A heart rate of 180 would therefore indicate a high level of stress in training. During recovery your HR will fall with time. How quickly it falls will depend upon how quickly the oxygen system can replenish the energy stores and restore normal equilibrium in your body. This depends upon a variety of factors including muscle capillarization and enzyme levels, all of which are an indication of your fitness. So the fitter you are the quicker your HR will return to normal. This is a well-known phenomenon in trained individuals.

Glycogen Stores and Phosphagen System

Aerobic glycolysis is the main process by which ATP is replenished although there may be some anaerobic glycolysis too. Either way, glycogen is broken down into carbon dioxide and water and the ATP is re-synthesised by a coupled reaction. So what? Well, this uses up glycogen during recovery. This glycogen has to be replaced between training sessions and this can take up to two days if a lot of glycogen has been used. You might conclude that increased glycogen stores in the muscles and liver would be helpful therefore, but you would be only partly right. More glycogen would enable you to perform more arduous and longer training sessions but it could be a hindrance in competition. This is because each glycogen molecule carries with it six water molecules and as a result you would feel bloated, heavy and slow. This is not what you want for an event lasting only a few seconds. If you want to feel light on your feet, springy and raring to go then do not place any emphasis on glycogen storage for sprint *events*. It is irrelevant. However, glycogen *is* important for *training*.

"How do I increase my glycogen stores?" I hear you ask. It's simple, eat and drink carbohydrates.

7.5 Variety in Training

Table 7.1 above should serve only as a guide for you. It indicates that high-quality practice with good quality rest relief is required if you are to train the phosphagen system successfully. Do not be afraid to take more rest if your recovery is not fast enough to enable you to achieve a high-quality performance in your next work bout. Quality is everything in the training of the phosphagen system. This can be achieved in many ways. The sprint followed by a walk back to the start, or whatever the equivalent of walk is in your sport. Or jog, sprint, jog, walk. Sprint, jog, sprint, walk. Jog, stride, sprint, jog, walk, rest. And so on. Variety is the spice of life and you should use your ingenuity to vary your routine, bearing in mind always two things:

1. That if you do anything new you run the risk of injuring yourself and so you must first condition yourself to the new activity.
2. You must overload yourself progressively to gain improvements.

112

8 TRAIN PAIN

As soon as ATP concentrations start to fall and ADP concentrations start to rise as a result of exercise, the process of anaerobic glycolysis swings into action. Glycogen is broken down to provide the energy for the resynthesis of ATP. The process leads to the production of pyruvate and what happens to the pyruvate depends on whether or not oxygen is available. Stored in the muscles is a tiny amount of oxygen, so some pyruvate will enter an energy releasing sequence known as the Krebs cycle and the electron transport system leading ultimately to the production of carbon dioxide and water with the further release of substantial energy.

However, after this small supply of oxygen stored in the muscles has been used up, if there is an inadequate supply of oxygen then the pyruvate will be converted to lactate instead. Inevitably, at the beginning of exercise the oxygen transport system has not yet woken up to the fact that there is a demand for oxygen so there is a shortage and lactate production is therefore a fact of life.

The rate of work will determine the rate of lactate production and also the response of the oxygen system. If the work rate is sufficiently low that the demand for oxygen can ultimately be met by supply then eventually after two to three minutes equilibrium will be reached and no more lactate will be produced.

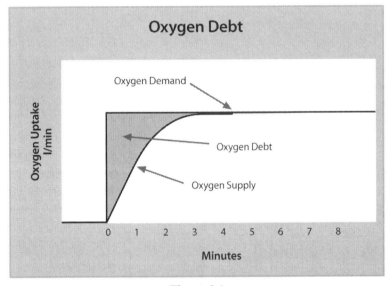

Figure 8.1

The oxygen debt is re-paid during recovery from exercise when oxygen supply exceeds the demand.

On the other hand if the work rate is so high that the oxygen supply can never meet the demand then lactate will continue to accumulate in the muscles and blood until, eventually, fatigue sets in and you have to stop working. Lactate actually inhibits further anaerobic glycolysis so that no more energy is released and work has to cease or fall to a level where the demand for oxygen can be met by the supply.

In maximal work periods exceeding 15 minutes the lactic acid system provides a relatively small proportion of the total energy required. However, in work periods under this time it becomes increasingly important being most predominant in events lasting between 1 and 4 minutes, see table in chapter 5.

Carbohydrate is the only fuel used by the lactic acid system.

8.1 Training the Lactic Acid System

Training the lactic acid system requires great mental toughness because it involves burning muscular pain, acute fatigue and breathlessness in combination with very high heart rates. You will be training the ability of your muscles to release energy from muscle glycogen stores in larger quantities than hitherto. This will lead to the production of greater quantities of lactic acid and so you have to train your body to tolerate these.

These changes take place largely in the fast twitch muscle fibres taking the form of increases in the activity of the specific enzymes used during anaerobic glycolysis. Because of the speed at which the training is undertaken there is an element of strength training involved leading to hypertrophy (enlargement) of the fast twitch fibres in particular.

8.2 Interval Training of the Lactic Acid System

Work designed to stress the lactic acid system should be longer in duration than that designed to stress the phosphagen system but not so long that the oxygen system plays a major role. Intervals of between 30 seconds and three minutes work duration should be the most effective, providing the opportunity for a great variety in the training diet.

Relief between intervals should include moderate work, which will partially inhibit the restoration of ATP and PC thus placing the emphasis upon anaerobic glycolysis for the provision of energy. The regulation of the relief interval can be governed by the heart rate HR. Typically, if the HR falls to 140 before work is re-started, recovery will be barely sufficient. Performance of the next work interval is likely to be at a lower intensity because the inhibitory effect of lactic acid will take effect sooner. If the heart rate is allowed to fall to 120 recovery will be more complete and it should be possible to perform several intervals at the same speed as the second interval. I say the second because the first is almost always faster if performed maximally simply because of the availability of ATP and PC. If the heart rate is allowed to fall to 100 then recovery is probably slightly too complete and ATP and PC may be nearly fully restored, although lactic acid will remain accumulated in the muscles and blood to some extent.

These heart rates are only rule of thumb guidelines to give you a feeling for what you might aim at if you are in your 20s.

Another rule of thumb is the three-minute recovery period. Really only below work periods of 1m 15s need this figure be reduced to two minutes or 1m 30s. Extending the recovery periods makes for greater emphasis on speed in each work bout. Reducing the recovery periods places more emphasis on the oxygen system and forces you to lower your work rate.

As I pointed out earlier, in no activity is the lactic acid system the sole source of energy. There is always an interplay with the phosphagen system or the oxygen system or both. The training dose table below is therefore split into training programmes that would emphasise the ATP - PC system and those that would emphasise the oxygen system.

TRAINING PRESCRIPTIONS FOR LACTIC ACID SYSTEM

Energy System	Work bout duration Min:Sec	Repetitions per set	Sets per training session	Rest between reps Min:Sec	Rest between sets (Min)
	0:30	5	5	1:30	5
ATP, PC, LA	0:40	5	4	2:00 - 2:30	6 - 7
	1:00 - 1:10	5	3	2:30 - 3:00	7 - 8
	1:20	5	2	3:00	8 - 10
	1:30 - 2:00	4	2	3:00	10 - 20
LA, O₂	2:10 - 2:40	6	1	3:00	-
	2:50 - 3:10	4	1	3:00	-

Table 8.1

The rest between sets is as important psychologically as it is physiologically. As I said earlier, this sort of training requires, and develops, mental toughness. Dividing the training into sets enables you to tackle a moderate chunk of very hard training at a time, in the knowledge that you may have a decent rest after a while. To face 20 or 25 intensive work bouts one after another is daunting task.

8.3 Work in Groups

The sort of interval training outlined above is easiest if tackled together with somebody else in a quasi-competitive situation. If your training partner is slower than you then give them a start. If you are slower then you should take a start. After one or two intervals it should be possible to arrive at a fairly accurate handicap.

If you are training in large groups then it might not be so important to have handicaps as there is most likely to be somebody of similar speed to you. If you have, or somebody else has, markedly greater or lesser talent, then by all means use a handicap. It does make for higher motivation and motivation is a necessary commodity in this type of hard training.

If racing against a training partner is not possible in your sport but lactic acid training, nevertheless, forms an important part of your training then you can still compete with each other but you have to be more creative.

If you are so good that nobody can get near to you in training you can compete against somebody with an advantage over you in some other form. A lesser swimmer for example could wear flippers in order to give you a race. A lesser athlete could cycle whilst you run. A canoeing crew in a K2, if of a lower ability than you might provide an ideal training partner for you in a K1. The opportunities to come up with creative solutions to your training problems are limitless. Remember don't accept the obvious.

8.4 The Penultimate Interval is the Hardest

If I didn't tell you this you would soon find out for yourself. Out of, say four intervals the first is usually the fastest and the last and second intervals are often of a similar but slower speed while the third is usually the slowest. The reason for this is almost certainly psychological in that you know that you dare not put everything into the penultimate interval. You would not then be able to work hard enough in the last interval to be able to finish in a blaze of glory that will leave you feeling good, although exhausted. However, in the final interval you know that you can have a proper rest afterwards so you are prepared to risk all! The first interval, of course, is fast for physiological reasons in that you have ATP and PC available, which in subsequent intervals is not in such plentiful supply.

Your objective should be to try to get each interval after the first one completed at exactly the same speed, say, 5 percent or 10 percent slower than the first interval.

8.5 Varying the Dose

Later when we come to programming you will see that not every day should be a hard day. The body needs to recover from training and this is particularly important in the run up to a competition. So you must be prepared to use a smaller dose than is outlined in each of the example training sessions in the table above. It is important that if a medium or light session is programmed that that is what you do and it is quite legitimate to halve or quarter the dosage indicated.

8.6 Start with Much Smaller Doses

In my training, which is year-round training, I do not do interval training at all times of the year. If I did I would soon get fed up with it. When the time comes to tackle it I find the prospect of wading into one of the full training sessions outlined above at the sort of intensity that I know I should be capable of, is far too daunting. So I break myself in gently, rebuilding my mental toughness as I go. I might tackle one interval first and then have more rest than I should whilst I summon up the courage to do another. Two might be all I can stomach first time out. I will gradually break myself into the training over a period of weeks building up the number of intervals and sets and reducing the relief periods progressively. I say progressively but a certain amount of randomness and doing as I feel helps to relieve the tedium of training and sometimes I will feel capable of more than I might have programmed for myself had it all been carefully structured. Once I have proved to myself that I can do it though, then the training must be structured and time-tabled so that I reach peak form on the right days.

8.7 Specificity in Lactic Acid Training

It is important to learn to perform well at the speed at which you will compete. To this end you will find it valuable in some of your training, particularly as you get closer to an important event, to follow the procedure adopted by the Danes in training their world champion lightweight sculler, Bjorn Eltang. If he had performed the usual six or eight 500m rows with only two minutes rest in between then the intensity would be too low. So he was asked to scull 500m as fast as possible, twice, taking 4 - 5 minutes to paddle back to the start for the second interval. During this paddle ATP and PC restoration would be inhibited but lactic acid would be transferred from the muscle tissue to the blood. At the end of the second 500m interval both muscle and blood would be loaded with lactate so a 15 minutes light paddle was used as work relief, to consume the lactate, before performing the same procedure again. Another 15-minute light paddle followed before the third and final set. During intensive training camps four sets might be undertaken.

This sort of training of the lactic acid system makes a lot of sense to me because the speed is above that at which normal competition over 2,000m would take place and we know that isokinetic training is speed specific. The training effect is largely at or below training speed rather than above the training speed so you need to train at adequate muscle contraction speeds.

8.8 Lactic Acid Removal

The normal resting concentration of lactic acid in the muscles is below one millimole per kg of muscle and yet in exhausting exercise this can rise to over 20mM/kg. It takes up to an hour and quarter for lactic acid concentration to return to normal if recovery takes the form of rest. However, if exercise of a low quality (say 50 percent of max VO_2) is performed during recovery then the lactic acid can be removed in about 20 minutes. This fits in with the quality oriented training pattern just outlined.

8.9 The Fate of Lactic Acid

Lactic acid may either be re-converted to glucose or glycogen in the liver or to glycogen in the muscle. But we know that the resynthesis of glycogen can take up to two days so there must be another, faster way of getting rid of lactic acid. It turns out that in the presence of oxygen lactic acid is first converted to pyruvic acid and then it can enter the Krebs cycle and the electron transport system yielding energy, carbon dioxide and water. This takes place mainly in the slow twitch fibres. So if moderate exercise is undertaken the lactic acid is actually used as a fuel by the working muscles. I stress the word moderate because if the work rate is too low you will approach the resting condition and the lactic acid will not been removed as quickly. There again if you work too hard you will generate more lactic acid thereby defeating the purpose of the work relicf. The work should be of a continuous nature rather than intermittent work because in intermittent work the intensity is usually too high and more lactate is produced.

The ability to remove lactic acid quickly is of great value, in particular when you have more than one competition in a day. Proper recovery will prevent that leaden feeling in your muscles when you go out to compete the second, third or fourth time.

8.10 Burning Out

Two to three months of serious, heavy lactic acid training is about as much as most athletes can bear. Results tend to be achieved very quickly and the variations in interval training that can be made would enable you to peak accurately for an important event. However it is all too easy to reach a peak too early in the season and become a spent force, seemingly unable to produce the goods. So if the world championships are in September and the season starts in May, do not be tempted to do too much of this sort of training in April. You may beat the world champion in June but the world champion is likely to beat you when it matters in September.

It is possible to peak twice in a season but I would advise you to revert to less intense work in between your peaks rather than trying to work progressively upwards from the first peak to the second using lactic acid training. Most coaches will conduct a revision period after selection, say and effectively go over again all the training that has been done through the preparation and pre-competition and competition periods. So a mini-season is fitted in between the qualification for the national team and the world championships.

8.11 Measuring Heart Rate

If you lay a long rope or hose pipe along the ground and flick one end up and down a wave or pulse will travel along the rope. Similarly when your heart beats it sends out a pressure wave or pulse which travels in the blood along the arteries. The speed that the pulse travels has nothing to do with the speed the blood is travelling at. Just as the speed that sound travels has nothing to do with the wind. If the arteries come close under the surface of the skin the pulse can be felt passing along. This is what you do to "take your pulse". The pulse rate is, of course, the same as your heart rate, HR. What you want to know is how many beats per minute your heart is making. Clearly during a minute your heart rate can change substantially, especially if you are exercising or recovering. Indeed it is actually changing all the time and no two inter-beat intervals are exactly the same. However, for our purposes it is sufficient to count the number of beats in six seconds and multiply by 10 or count the number of beats in 10 seconds and multiply by six. The former is probably easier. So if you count 12 beats then your HR is 12 x 10 = 120.

Be careful always to start counting with the word "nought" or you will count a beat too many.

Figure 8.2

A thoughtful study of the watch face shown here using the example of 12 beats in six seconds (two beats per second) should reveal why. If you start counting with the word "one" when the second hand is at the top then you will reach the number 13 by the sixth second. Multiplication of 13 by 10 gives you a HR of 130 and yet clearly at this rate it is impossible for 130 beats to have taken place by the time the second hand returns to starting position.

Many people find it difficult to find their pulse so that they can measure it. If you are one then may I suggest that you do some strenuous exercise first to get the heart beating more strongly? Then your pulses are much easier to find. Here are some places to search for an easy pulse to find.

On the wrist at the base of the thumb, not in the middle of the wrist.

At the temple just in front of your ear but behind your side burns if you have any.

On the carotid artery which is to the left of your windpipe.

To find this last one hold your head up straight and take a gentle hold of your wind pipe with your right hand placing your thumb on the right side and your fingers on the left side of your throat. Found it? Don't worry if you haven't. It took me ages to discover this one. The trick is to make sure your head is stretched up. Once you have found it you will find that you can trace the path of the artery up quite far until it disappears under your jaw. Of course, a fairly obvious place to feel your heartbeat is on your chest where the heart will be visibly pounding away during and immediately following exercise. It is not so easy to find during rest, however, so get used to using other pulses.

My favourite pulse is on the temple because I can feel it in my head as well as my finger and the feedback to the mechanisms that control my heartbeat feels more direct. I will come to the value of this later in psychological training.

Of course, nowadays HR monitors are cheap and mostly they are reliable so their use has become commonplace. There are many guides to training with HR monitors but beware. HR monitors can limit your performance. It is easy to become obsessed with HR and to put incorrect limits on your training and upon your speed in competition. Some top coaches now encourage their athletes to throw their HR monitors away!

9 GASP

In the introduction to the lactic acid energy system I explained that as soon as work begins and ATP concentrations in the muscle fall the process of anaerobic glycolysis begins. Now if oxygen is present then the pyruvate, which results from this energy releasing process, can enter the Krebs cycle and the electron transport system, releasing even more energy. In fact if oxygen is present a lot more energy is released from the breakdown of glycogen, 13 times as much altogether! However the rate at which it is released is unfortunately lower than the rate at which energy may be released by anaerobic glycolysis so the lactic acid system must be used if high speeds are desired.

The Krebs cycle and electron transport system is capable of using another fuel apart from pyruvate. Fat can be turned into carbon dioxide and water in the presence of oxygen with the release of large quantities of energy. Again though, the rate of release of energy from fats is lower by approximately 13 percent than it is from pyruvate so at fast aerobic speeds carbohydrate is the preferred fuel whereas at slow speeds fats may be used in increasing proportion.

Fats are an incredibly efficient store of energy in terms of the amount of energy stored for a given weight. They carry about six to seven times the amount of energy that the equivalent weight of glycogen would carry so obviously the body likes to store energy in this way and fortunately the body knows how to release the stored energy easily and quickly. We will return to fat metabolism later. For the time being, though, we will confine ourselves to the consideration of work that is of sufficient intensity that only aerobic glycolysis takes place, that is the breakdown of glycogen in the presence of oxygen.

9.1 Oxygen Uptake

An awful lot of information is available about the aerobic energy system because it has been studied extensively. One of the most important findings has been that when a steady state has been reached the amount of oxygen consumed is directly proportional to the work rate, see diagram. A steady state means that the oxygen uptake is constant and a state of equilibrium exists between the supply of and demand for oxygen.

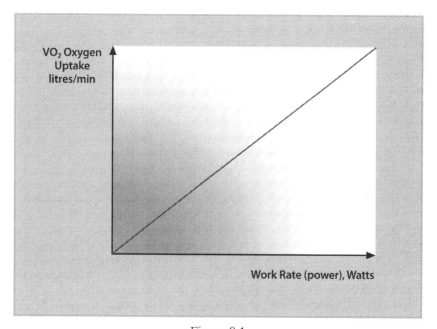

Figure 9.1

The slope of the line is different from one individual to another and even from one activity to another in the same individual. However, given that one individual does one thing such as cycling on a cycle ergometer then there is this straight line relationship between the power output of the individual and the oxygen input known as VO_2. The V stands for volume and there should be a dot over it indicating the rate of change of the volume with respect to time but this is frequently omitted. VO_2 is measured in litres per minute but in some sports it is more useful to express it in terms of body weight as well. So if you are working with a VO_2 of three litres per minute and you weigh 75 kg then your VO_2 may be expressed as:

3/75k = 40 ml / kg / minute

9.2 Heart Rate and Oxygen Uptake

The next interesting and useful thing that has been discovered about the aerobic system is that HR is directly proportional to oxygen uptake.

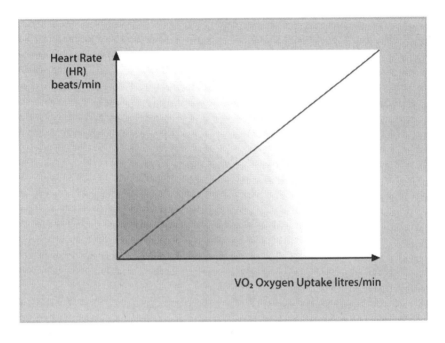

Figure 9.2

This means that as long as a steady state has been reached and as long as you are not working anaerobically then your HR will also be directly proportional to your work rate.

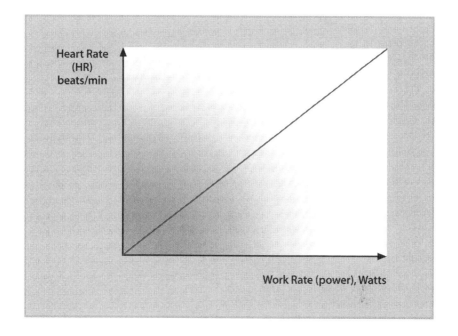

Figure 9.3

This means that you can tell how hard you are working aerobically by monitoring your heart rate. Remember that it takes two to three minutes to achieve steady state conditions following a change in demand for oxygen. This is the case in changing from rest to work or if simply increasing the work rate.

9.3 Max HR and MaxVO$_2$

Your HR cannot go on and on increasing. Eventually a limit is reached and the heart is unable to beat any faster. The limit is *approximately* 220 minus your age. It follows, simplistically, that when your maximum HR is reached in steady state conditions then so is your maximum oxygen uptake. So there is a limit to how much oxygen your body can use per minute and consequently there is a limit to your aerobic power. Exceed this limit and the extra power has to be generated anaerobically. If you work anaerobically lactic acid will be produced and it is only a question of time before you have to stop owing to fatigue.

The maximum oxygen uptake, max VO$_2$, is therefore a key factor in endurance events and there are numerous statistics to show that the higher your max VO$_2$ the better your endurance performance is likely to be.

9.4 Resting Metabolism

At the bottom end of the scale, of course, are the resting conditions and needless to say resting heart rate is not zero and neither is resting VO_2 because there is a metabolic cost just to staying alive. This is typically 3.5 ml O_2 / kg / min and clearly the lower your HR is in this resting condition the more efficient is your oxygen transport system. So resting HR is an indicator (and only and indicator) of aerobic fitness. In normal adults resting HR would be between 70 and 80 beats per minute (usually higher for women). Very fit people may go as low as 50 beats per minute at rest but the very top class endurance athletes have resting heart rates in the 30s! I know an Olympic medal winning rower with a resting heart rate of 36 and a cyclist whose resting heart rate was 32. The cyclist wore a special tag on his wrist in case he was involved in an accident so that any doctor attempting to diagnose what was wrong with him would know that in his case such a low HR was not abnormal.

9.5 Typical Values for Max VO₂

The average male 20 year old would have a Max VO_2 of 35 to 40ml O_2/kg/min whilst an average fit male between 20 and 30 years old would have a Max VO_2 of between 40 and 50ml O_2/kg/min. The maximum aerobic power of females is about 15 to 20 percent lower than males except at the younger ages, up to about 13, where the difference is negligible.

The aerobic power necessary to be able to complete a mile in four minutes is 70ml O_2/kg/min. Athletes of Seb Coe's calibre can be expected to have a Max VO_2 of the order of 90ml O_2/kg/min. Whilst you can readily see that this is exceptionally high you should also note that in the average athlete it is only possible to increase max VO_2 by about 20 percent through training. What improvement you can achieve depends upon how far along the training road you have already got. But clearly if you are not born with sufficient natural talent to be within striking distance then you are unlikely to become a world champion.

Do not despair. There is only one world champion in each event and the odds are heavily stacked against all of us if that is what we aspire to. Yet many, many people who are not world champions can and do consider themselves to be successful competitors. So read on.

9.6 Training the Oxygen System
Interval Training

To train the oxygen system you need to put it under stress. Now we know that it takes two to three minutes from rest to reach the steady state where the oxygen supply equals demand so conventionally training work periods must be at least that long. We also know that it is not possible to work continuously at your maximum oxygen uptake. In fact about 4-10 minutes would be the most that you could endure working at your Max VO_2, six minutes being a more likely upper limit. This is because in order to reach your Max VO_2 you have to cross your anaerobic threshold, more of which later, and then the anaerobic system plays an increasing part in the supply of energy until so much lactic acid is produced that you have to stop work. If you want to be able to continue working aerobically for long periods then you must stay under your anaerobic threshold. In other words because of the overlap between the different energy systems it is impossible to reach your maximum aerobic power without substantially recruiting the lactic acid system to provide some energy.

So getting back to the training of your maximum oxygen uptake it would appear that periods of work between three and five minutes would be optimal for stressing your maximum oxygen uptake. With suitable rest periods you will be able to reach your maximum oxygen uptake several times in one training session. The relief periods should be rest relief so that you do not stress the lactic acid system when you are trying to stress the oxygen system. Again the three-minute rule of thumb can be used to determine the rest period or else the HR can be monitored as before. For athletes in their 20s starting work again when the HR has fallen to 120 should not prove to be too stressful whereas starting when it has fallen only to 140 is likely to lead to a slowing down during the latter intervals. If you are training in a group you will usually find that there is a time when everybody's heart rates are between 120 and 140 and so it is possible to start the next interval together.

INTERVAL TRAINING DOSAGE FOR TRAINING THE OXYGEN SYSTEM

Major Energy System	Training Time Min:Sec	Repetitions per set	Sets per session	Relief Time Min:Sec	Type of Relief
ATP - PC - O_2	0:30	10	3	0:15	Light Work
LA - O_2	3:00	5	1	3:00	Rest
O_2	4:00	4	1	3:00	Rest
O_2	5:	3	1	3:00	Rest

Table 9.1

Just as it is possible to improve your strength without lifting maximal weights or putting yourself under undue stress, so it is possible to improve your maximum oxygen uptake without reaching your maximal oxygen uptake. As long as you use your oxygen system it will improve. However the amount and rate of improvement does depend upon the intensity of the training. This is particularly important as you approach the limit of your natural talent and the law of diminishing returns comes into play. I will touch on this again when I explain how to design your training program.

It is also possible to work at a rate substantially below the maximum you can endure for, say, four minutes and yet still reach your maximum oxygen uptake. This means that training the oxygen system should be quite pleasant especially when compared to training the lactic acid system. In fact it is desirable that the effort should not be maximal. It has been shown that in some cases during maximal efforts the oxygen uptake and other factors such as the amount of blood the heart pumps out per minute (the cardiac output) have been below their maximal levels.

Also the presence of high levels of lactic acid in the body appears to be deleterious to Max VO_2 performance. A useful way of achieving your VO_2 Max without having too much lactate is to sprint (sub-maximally) for 30 seconds, then have 15 seconds light work relief and do 10 of these repetitions in each of three sets, separating each set by three to five minutes of rest relief. Breathing will be heavy and HR high but lactate (and pain) will be relatively low.

Continuous Work

The fact that you do not have to reach your max VO_2 to have an effect on it means that you can introduce other types of work into your training program to train the oxygen system. Before considering other alternatives, first we should envisage the oxygen uptake system as divided into two parts:

The oxygen **transport** system, the heart, lungs and the blood and the major blood vessels

The oxygen **utilisation** system, the capillaries, the muscles, mitochondria and enzymes.

Moderate Duration Steady State

Training the oxygen transport system demands a high volume stress on the heart and lungs and blood vessels and this is achieved at high heart rates over periods of around 30 minutes. This is often referred to as anaerobic threshold, AT, training because it is the sort of duration of exercise that can be performed at your anaerobic threshold. It should not be confused with training designed to improve the anaerobic threshold, which is of a lower intensity and longer duration.

Long Duration Steady State

Training the oxygen *utilisation* system requires that only the slow twitch, type I and the type IIa muscle fibres are recruited. This means that the appropriate changes take place in these fibres, as this is where the oxygen is utilised. To be sure that only these fibres are recruited the intensity must be kept low and the duration long. Utilisation 1 training can be sustained for about an hour whereas Utilisation 2 training would normally last for one and a half hours or even more. As utilisation training is undertaken at a steady state, it does not appear stressful at the outset. Only towards the end of a training session are you likely to feel any distress. This would normally be due to muscular fatigue caused by depleted glycogen stores. It should not be due to the accumulation of lactic acid, which is a different sort of stress altogether. Utilisation training does improve the anaerobic threshold even though it is performed at intensities that are significantly below the anaerobic threshold.

Clearly almost any form of the aerobic activity can be used to train the oxygen **transport** system, running, swimming, canoeing, rowing, cross-country skiing, circuit training, aerobics, cycling. This is where cross training can help to provide you with some variety in your training diet.

However, oxygen **utilisation** training is muscle specific as it is only in the muscles that the utilisation takes place and it is only in the muscles that beneficial training effects can be brought about. This has clear implications for your training program. There is not much point in using circuit training in an attempt to provide yourself with Utilisation 2 training for 1.5 hours. Utilisation training must be sport specific. Use your circuit training for oxygen transport training by all means.

At the upper limits of endurance at a slow pace you will run into fuel supply problems. Here you will not be training the oxygen system effectively, as what will be holding you back is a shortage of fuel, not a shortage of oxygen. It is important, therefore to use mainly fat (of which you have plenty) as your fuel, and to do this intensity must be kept low.

Over-distance Training

Working just below the competition pace for a period just a little longer than the competition period is over-distance work. You work just over the distance you will race, say one and a half times the race distance, if racing is what you are training for. This could be repeated between one and four times depending on your freshness, the intensity of the pace at which each work interval is performed and the overall intended intensity of the training session. If you are intending that today's over-distance training session should be a light one then you might only do one bout of work and make it non-too fast either. A fairly typical over-distance session might be 3 x 10 min with 3 - 10 min rest relief for somebody whose normal race distance would last, say, 6 - 7 minutes.

Tempo Training

If you are intending to race in a competition where you will be working in such a way that you have to spread your effort - this can be anything from running 200m to swimming the channel - then it is important to be able to lock on straight away to the correct pace. This is particularly important where the anaerobic systems and aerobic systems overlap and both play important roles. The trick here is to spread the build-up of lactic acid correctly over the race so that exhaustion is reached only on the finishing line and not before. Tempo training is of great value here. You learn to perform at the right tempo. It usually takes the form of two repetitions of approximately 3/4 to 7/8 of the race distance with substantial recovery between. The work is performed exactly at race pace. Because you are not going to whole distance, psychologically you are able to cope with performance at race pace which otherwise (over the full distance) you would be unable to do in training and would normally only be able to do in a competitive situation. This sort of training is used towards the end of an annual training cycle, as the big competitions approach, during the final tuning period when the training becomes exceptionally specific.

Even Splits

In tempo training in particular you should be aiming to achieve perfectly even split times over various fractions of the total distance. You will find that the top athletes, be they swimmers, runners, rowers, whatever are able to achieve split times to within tenths or even hundredths of a second of each other. A truly remarkable feat. You must aim to be able to do this. You should also experiment with bursts of pace at various stages in order to determine how you would feel if you chose to try and beat an opponent in the middle of a race instead of at the end. Usually when you see somebody apparently being beaten by a burst of speed in the middle of a race they are actually moving slower because they went too fast to start with. The winner is not in fact going substantially faster but is really going at the same even pace when others are fading. Conversely, somebody who does actually go fast in the middle of a race in order to burn off his opponents runs the risk of accumulating too much lactic acid too soon, being unable to maintain his pace and finally being passed again before the finish. It is such tactics that provide all the drama in middle and long distance events.

Alternate Training

This is a form of training where steady state activity alternates with work of higher intensity. After a few repetitions lactic acid would accumulate to the point where light work recovery has to be undertaken to allow a further set to be done. A typical training session might take the form of two minutes fast followed by two minutes at a steadier pace repeated four times in each of two sets with five minutes of light work between the sets. It is usual after the fourth fast repetition to omit the fourth steady pace peace and go straight into light work to recover.

It is all too easy, especially in a competitive training situation, for this sort of training to degenerate into intensive intervals with the fast work periods becoming flat out pieces and the steady pace deteriorating into light work. This is not what is intended. The idea is that working close to the anaerobic threshold, the anaerobic threshold can be pushed closer to the maximum oxygen uptake. Sadly, there is no evidence to suggest that this is actually what happens as a result of this type of training.

9.7 The Anaerobic Threshold

I have mentioned this enough times now to have aroused your curiosity, I am sure. It is an important concept to grasp as it is a performance-limiting factor that can be altered by training. If we plot blood lactate against oxygen uptake we find that there is a linear relationship, a straight line. So the harder you work the greater the concentration of lactate in the blood.

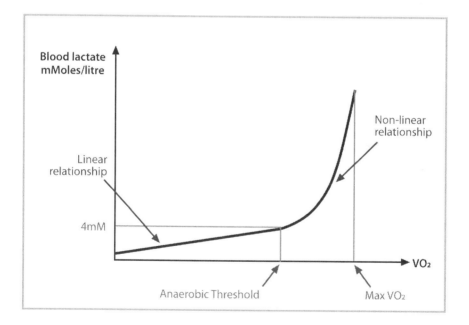

Figure 9.4

There comes a point on the graph, however, where the proportionality ceases. The straight line bends (usually at about 4 millimoles per litre), and instead of a given increase in work rate giving rise to the same increase in the lactate as before, now instead there is a disproportionately large increase in the lactate concentration. This is the anaerobic threshold and is the point at which it is thought that anaerobic glycolysis begins to supply an increasing proportion of the energy requirement, even though the oxygen system is not yet fully stretched.

You can see from the figure that the anaerobic threshold can be expressed as a percentage of your max VO_2, say 65% in this case. If you are going to work for a long time then you dare not cross your anaerobic threshold because the lactic acid will accumulate and you will have to slow down again. So your anaerobic threshold is an important factor in endurance events and the nearer it is to your max VO_2 the greater the proportion of your maximal aerobic power you will be able to use. It is important also in middle distance events because the higher your anaerobic threshold the faster that you can go before anaerobic processes need to be called upon to provide energy, leaving you with a greater reserve of anaerobic power. The next figure gives you an idea of the result you are attempting to achieve from your training.

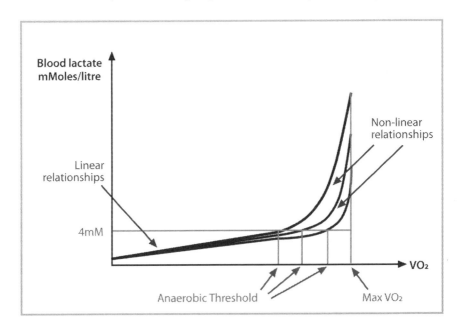

Figure 9.5

Highly trained athletes may have anaerobic thresholds in the region of 90 - 95% of their Max VO_2.

The question arises, "How do I know when I am at my anaerobic threshold?" It would be unreasonable to expect you to run around with a catheter in a vein all the time so blood samples may be taken. Fortunately there is something else that happens at the anaerobic threshold that with practice you may readily detect. At low work rates there is a similar linear relationship between oxygen uptake and breathing rate but when the anaerobic threshold is crossed the breathing rate increases disproportionately. Experienced performers are able to detect this point quite easily and use it, often subconsciously, to control their pace in endurance events. In other words there is a feedback loop in operation here. If you bring your awareness of breathing rate from the subconscious to the conscious you also learn where your anaerobic threshold is. By listening to your opponent's breathing when running alongside another competitor you may detect if he/she has crossed his/her anaerobic threshold and this can help you with tactics.

It used to be thought that *shifting* the anaerobic threshold could be achieved by training *at* the anaerobic threshold i.e. with lactate concentrations of 4 mmol/l. But more recent research has shown that this pace cannot be maintained for more than about 45 minutes and that concentrations of 2.5 mmol/l are more typical amongst athletes doing large volumes of endurance training. Only by keeping the intensity this low are athletes able to train as much as five hours per day. The higher the intensity the quicker the glycogen stores run out. Training continuously at 4 mmol/l would deplete them in one hour. By training at low intensities you recruit the slow twitch, Type I muscle fibres and you burn fat rather than glycogen. It is in these fibres that the necessary changes take place to shift your anaerobic threshold.

10 FUEL SUPPLY LIMITATION

So far we have discovered that endurance performance is limited by maximum oxygen uptake and also limited by the anaerobic threshold which determines what proportion of your max VO_2 is usable for long periods. But there is another limitation, the fuel supply. At work rates that are high enough to tax the lactic acid system the fuel used is carbohydrate in the form of glycogen stored in the muscles and liver and glucose in the blood and liver. The longer the duration of an event the greater is the use of fat as a fuel. In fact one of the features associated with increased fitness is an increase in fat metabolism at a given submaximal workload. However, we know that the rate of energy release from fat metabolism is about 13 percent lower than the rate of release of energy from carbohydrate metabolism so it is possible to perform faster for longer if carbohydrate is used as the fuel. Unfortunately there is a limited supply of carbohydrate, glycogen, in the body. It is stored mainly in the muscles, where, of course, it will be used, and there is only enough under normal circumstances to last for about 1.5 hours before deterioration in performance can be detected. After 4 hours it is usually all gone.

It is even more unfortunate that "fat only burns in the carbohydrate fire" so although the average body stores enough fat for 1000 hours of low grade work, a work rate of 15 percent below the anaerobic threshold cannot even be maintained once the glycogen has run out.

This phenomenon, glycogen depletion, only ever affected me when I performed very long endurance events lasting 4-5 hours, such as the Boston marathon, a rowing event in England between Lincoln and Boston. Once, I was forced by circumstance into a situation where I was not able to eat properly either the evening before the event or the morning of the event. After two hours I started to slow down. By 3.5 hours people had passed me who had never beaten me before and when I found myself unable to keep up with a young teenaged girl I just ground to a halt. A schoolmaster supporting his own crew came to my rescue with a Mars bar and a drink of orange squash. Within minutes I was back up to full speed and quickly passed the young girl again. I was even complemented upon the speed of my finish but the race was lost by then, all because I had run out of fuel.

On another occasion, a girl I was coaching, after a two-week layoff following an operation, decided on Wednesday that she was fit for a race on Saturday. She came to this conclusion because on the Wednesday she beat her training partner by 10 seconds in a 25-minute race following a 35-minute warm up. However, in the race on Saturday over the same course with the same warm up she was unable to repeat the performance. In fact this time her training partner beat her by 10 seconds. After the race she felt so weak she could hardly stand up and she felt nauseous (sick) and dizzy.

What had happened? In fact she was suffering from hypoglycaemia, a shortage of blood sugar, which affects the nervous system when it is acute. Why was this? Simple. Unbeknown to me she had been dieting ever since her operation. The Wednesday training session had depleted her meagre glycogen stores and she had not replaced them by eating properly on Thursday and Friday so she was short of fuel.

I was perplexed at the time, thinking that the poor performance was perhaps psychological. It was not until I asked what she had been eating that I realised the cause. It just goes to show how careful you have to be in controlling all sorts of factors including diet and "dieting" if you are going to win when you want to.

10.1 How to Increase Your Glycogen Stores

Increasing the amount of glycogen stored in the muscles will enable you to sustain your speed for longer. At the work rate above 75 percent of your max VO_2 you will normally be exhausted after 1.5 hours. With extra glycogen on-board this time can be extended to 2.5 or even 4 hours depending on the method used. This has obvious implications for marathon runners. It explains in a physiological way the existence of the "the wall", a barrier to normal progress at around 20 miles. It should be noted that the extra glycogen does not make you go faster anymore than putting extra petrol in a car makes it go faster, it merely extends your endurance. So if you are not competing for longer than about 1.5 hours it is not worth "glycogen loading". Nevertheless it is as well to be aware that one long, steady state, training session or three days hard interval training can sufficiently deplete your glycogen stores to impair your performance quite seriously.

You may increase your glycogen stores simply by eating more carbohydrates. If you do a lot of heavy training you will need to have a high carbohydrate diet anyway. Recovery days where more fuel is taken on-board than you use up are an essential feature for the heavily training athlete to prevent the quality of work undertaken from suffering. Remember intensity is the most important factor in training. Two to three days of a high carbohydrate diet will have a substantial effect

The body will absorb more carbohydrate if it is first starved of it. So preceding a high carbohydrate diet with a high protein and fat diet, low in carbohydrate is a way to load even more carbohydrate. The whole process can be done in 4-5 days.

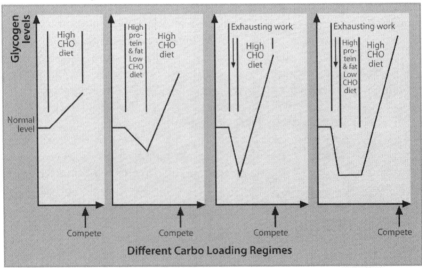

Different Carbo Loading Regimes

Figure 10.1

136

Whilst on the high protein and fat diet, especially if you are training hard still, you will find a tendency to become fatigued and irritable so it is as well to forewarn work mates, family and friends in case this happens to you. Don't use it as an excuse to bite people's heads off though. That would be unreasonable.

The ultimate refinement in "Carbo-loading" involves first of all a depletion of the glycogen stores by performing a long duration training session. The depletion may be followed by either of the two loading processes outlined above. You may either eat carbohydrates straight away or put yourself on a fat and protein diet for 2-3 days first then eat a high carbohydrate diet for further 3-4 days. So a week is needed for this latter procedure. This is probably only necessary for very long endurance events taking over three hours to complete.

10.2 Specificity of Loading

Experiments involving the depletion of glycogen stores by exhaustive exercise on only one leg followed by a high carbohydrate diet have shown that the super-compensation only takes place in the muscles of the exercised leg. This shows two things.

- That depletion facilitates loading.
- Loading is specific to the muscle depleted.

So it is important to realise that it is no use swimming to exhaustion if the event you are going to compete in for over 1.5 hours is a running event. Tri-athletes have a problem here in that they have to swim, cycle and run. Their event lasts more than 1.5 hours and glycogen loading is an appropriate course of action to take to improve endurance. The problem is the variety of muscles used and which ones to load. I would contend that a Tri-athlete should do a triathlon in order to deplete exactly the correct muscles to the appropriate degree. It is possible then to do a triathlon every week with the correct diet and each event provides the training for the next event. This regime is popular with racers of endurance events of all types who would find that without racing training becomes drudgery but that with both heavy training and racing the racing performances deteriorate rather than improve.

10.3 What does it feel like?

Every glycogen molecule carries with it six molecules of water so when you have loaded up with glycogen you feel bloated and heavy. You do not feel sparkling and bouncy and you should not expect to. If you do a sport where you have to lift your own body weight up and down continually you will not notice any benefit from "Carbo-loading" until about two hours into your competition. This is clearly the case with running and is a good reason why you should not load too much if you are only running a half marathon.

Injury or some other reason for an enforced layoff from heavy training can lead you to Carbo-load unwittingly. Upon returning to training you may feel this heaviness and it may affect your performance, positively in terms of long duration endurance training but perhaps negatively if fast work is attempted. It is well to be aware of this effect.

10.4 Vitamins and Carbo-loading

There is a danger with some high carbohydrate diets that you may not get enough of the essential vitamins and trace elements in your diet. Niacin has been mentioned in particular as a coenzyme essential to the proper function of the Krebs cycle. A reduced max VO_2 may result if you are not careful. So take care to consume complex carbohydrates and try to avoid refined foods such as sugar in your diet. Wholemeal bread, pasta and rice with plenty of fresh fruit and vegetables should form the basis of your high carbohydrate diet.

10.5 Intake of Fluids before and during Exercise.

The Urine Check

It is essential for the body to have sufficient water on-board before competition. The way to tell is to check your urine. If it is yellow and cloudy then you do not have enough water whereas if it is pale and clear, you do.

Before Competition

Do not fall into the trap of taking glucose or sweet drinks or boiled sweets immediately before a race in the hope that this will improve your performance. The body detects the increase in blood sugar and the pancreas starts pumping out insulin in order to bring the concentrations back to normal. The result is that within fifteen minutes there is actually less, not more, available blood sugar and this could in fact lead to a poorer performance rather than a better one. It is best to drink up to a pint of water, no later than 30 minutes before competition.

Fizzy Drinks and Sweet Drinks

Replacing energy consumed during exercise is a different matter especially if you have further competitions later in the day. Sweet Drinks may be in order here but try to avoid fizzy, carbonated ones. The dissolved carbon dioxide in them will only have to be disposed of by the body and as carbon dioxide is a by-product of exercise anyway the body already has its work cut out. Sweetness should not be higher than 2.5g/100ml or absorption will be inhibited and the liquid will linger in the stomach. This is approximately 1/4 teaspoon of sugar per cup of water. In the long endurance events the choice of whether to drink "Energy Drinks" or water depends largely upon the main method of cooling of the body (see hyperthermia). If water is being lost through sweating then it is more important to replace this water than it is to replenish the glycogen stores.

Salt Tablets

It should not be necessary to take salt tablets when you lose a lot of fluid by sweating. The reason for this is that sweat has a lower concentration of salt in it than the normal body fluids which means that the fluid lost is largely water and the concentration of salt in the remaining body fluid will already be above normal. Adding salt would therefore make matters worse, not better. Drinking water is much more important. Only when in extremely hot conditions where vast quantities of water are consumed to replace vast quantities of sweat lost would it be necessary to take extra salt. Even then it need not be much as we are advised that we already take too much salt in our daily diet than is good for us.

Drinking during Exercise

If, during a long endurance event, you wait until you are thirsty before you drink then you have left it too late. You should drink approximately one cup of water every 10 to 15 minutes throughout prolonged activity. Also afterwards you should continue drinking more than thirst demands because if you rely on thirst alone it could take you up to two days to replace lost water.

10.6 The Consequences of Failure Regulate Body Temperature

If you get too cold you suffer from hypothermia. If you get too hot you suffer from hyperthermia. In extreme cases death ensues but there are symptoms you can detect in order to prevent death and there are things you can do to prevent even the symptoms arising and to cure them once they have arisen.

Hypothermia - Exposure

Prolonged exposure to cold conditions without adequate protective clothing leads first of all to a constriction of the blood vessels under the skin so as to minimise heat loss. This is followed by shivering, which can increase the metabolism by 50 percent, furnishing heat as a by-product. Heavy exercise can increase the metabolism by several times but if sweating starts this can dampen clothing. Wet clothing has heat conductivity 80 times that of dry clothing so when you stop exercising and cool down it is essential to change into warm dry clothing if possible.

Because the brain needs plenty of oxygen there is a substantial blood supply to the head no matter how cold it gets. This means that excessive amounts of heat can be lost from the body in very cold conditions if a hat is not worn, but it also means that the onset of sweating can be delayed by the removal of a hat during heavy exercise. The head is an effective radiator.

The symptoms are hypothermia include falling behind (in a walking party, say) and delirium. Sometimes shivering ceases and if the subject is asleep he or she may object to being disturbed. The *cure* is the removal of damp or wet clothing and replacement with warm dry clothing followed by the gradual raising of the body core temperature. This can be done by getting into a sleeping bag with the patient and using your own body heat to warm them, or if a warm bath or shower is available this can be used. Care must be taken not to use a temperature that is too high and also not to provide drinks that are too hot. Naturally, medical assistance should be sought as soon as possible. Alcohol should NOT be given.

Hyperthermia - Heat Stroke (Sun Stroke)
Heat is lost from the body by **convection** e.g. wind. If there is no wind or if you are, say, running with the wind, convection all but ceases and other methods of heat loss come into play. Cooling by convection is the main method of heat loss in cycling and skiing where effectively wind speeds are high. Also in swimming, provided the water is not too warm.

Radiation is the route by which most heat is lost from the resting individual at normal room temperature. However if the environmental temperature rises to the same temperature as the body then radiation ceases and if the surrounding temperature is higher than body temperature then radiation takes place in the opposite direction and heat is absorbed by the body instead of lost. This is particularly so on clear, hot, sunny afternoons. It is possible, however, to absorb heat from the sun by radiation even when the air temperature is cold and provided there is no wind you may find yourself sweating in order to dissipate this unwelcome heat.

Conduction is the method of heat transmission when you touch something. Whether heat is lost or gained depends upon the temperature of what you touch and its conductivity.

Cooling by *evaporation* is the major method of heat loss during heavy exercise, especially at low speeds where cooling by convection is slight if not non-existent. As sweat reaches the surface of the skin the highest energy water molecules escape into the atmosphere leaving behind the lower energy molecules. Molecules with low energy have a low temperature so the evaporation of high-energy molecules leaves behind a cooling liquid on the surface of skin. Looking at it another way the heat energy within the body is transported into the atmosphere by the evaporating molecules.

In running, where the whole body weight has to be supported and the work load is high but relative wind speeds are low, cooling by evaporation plays a major role so water replacement is all the more essential. It is possible to gain occasional extra cooling and temporary relief from heat stress by increasing the surface area of your body that is exposed. This can only be achieved by opening the fist and spreading the fingers or by raising the elbows enough to allow air to circulate around the armpits without unduly affecting your running technique.

Problems occur with cooling by evaporation in conditions of high humidity when there are so many water molecules already in the air that it is saturated with them and there is no room for any more. Then cooling by evaporation fails and you are left wet with sweat, having to resort to cold drinks that pass through the body producing warm urine. If temperatures are very high and sweating is profuse urination may cease.

You can see from the above discussion that adequate water intake is essential in maintaining heat balance. If you are unable to keep your temperature down you will find that your endurance is impaired. You may be able to work maximally but not for as long as if you had a normal temperature. At submaximal workloads your heart's stroke volume (the amount of blood pumped in one beat) will fall and heart rate will have to rise to compensate.

In conditions of very low humidity it is possible to lose considerable body fluid by insensible sweating (sweating without being aware of it) because the evaporation takes place as soon as the sweat reaches the surface of the skin. The standard urine test will reveal this.

Prevention and Cure of Hyperthermia

Athletes are particularly vulnerable to heat cramps, heat exhaustion and finally heat stroke because they are highly motivated individuals and liable to over extend themselves. Add to this the use of heavy protective clothing as in, say, American football, which prevents heat loss by evaporation, together with the ignorance of the importance of water intake on the part of the athlete or worse still the coach or worse even than that the competition organisers and you have a potentially lethal combination. IT SHOULD BE CLEAR THAT PREVENTION OF HEAT DISORDERS IS USUALLY POSSIBLE BY THE SIMPLE EXPEDIENT OF DRINKING ADEQUATELY. First aid cure is simple too, requiring immediate removal of all clothing and cooling by whatever method possible, hose, iced water, cold showers. Again medical attention should be sought quickly. As the gut has difficulty in absorbing water rapidly, it should be taken on-board in small very frequent doses. If glucose or sugar is added to the water it will be absorbed *less* easily so on hot days concentrate on water first and energy second.

A friend once described to me a foolish encounter with the sun. Upon his return from a long walk on a sunny beach he was as red as a lobster and "could feel his blood boiling". Fortunately he knew what to do and sat under a cold shower for as long as it took to get his temperature down, emerging only to collect cold cans of Coke from the refrigerator periodically. Being bald he was left a souvenir of this close call: the skin of his scalp which peeled off in one piece. It's true! He showed it to me.

10.7 Temperature and Performance

There is evidence to support the theory that proper warming up improves sprint performance. Sprinters also like warm conditions. Apart from anything else the likelihood of injury is lower when it is warm than when it is hot. Also fluid viscosity is lower when warm so the resistance provided by warm air or by warm water is lower than when it is cold.

Endurance athletes on the other hand do not like warm conditions. There is little chance of setting a marathon record when it is warm. The reason for this is that some of the blood has to be used to transport heat from where it is generated in the muscles to the surface of the skin where it can be dissipated. This means that fractionally less blood is available for the transport of oxygen to the muscles.

10.8 Blood Donors

Haemoglobin carries oxygen in the blood from the lungs, where it picks it up, to those parts of the body that need it. The more haemoglobin you have in your blood the higher your oxygen carrying capacity and the higher your maximum oxygen uptake may be. If you give blood you lose some of your haemoglobin with the red blood cells that are removed with the blood. Whilst the blood volume is replaced quickly by the body the red blood cells take some time, about a month, to be replaced from bone marrow. So in the mean time you will have a reduced max VO_2, impaired performance and a higher than expected heart rate at submaximal work loads.

This effect manifested itself quite clearly in a step test that I did on a girl once. As she was one of the fittest in the group I expected the heart rate to be amongst the lowest immediately after the test but it was the highest, 172. A quick calculation based on the effect of losing 13.5% of her estimated blood volume revealed that she would have had a HR of 152 and this would, in fact, have been amongst the lowest.

During the period when the red blood cells are being restored to normal concentration it is probable that the quality of work possible in training will not be high enough to maintain or improve performance.

10.9 Altitude

There is a similar problem in training at altitude and occasional trips to sea level for high-quality training sessions should be undertaken during a high altitude training camp. The effects of altitude training are well known. The exposure to low atmospheric pressure and therefore low levels of oxygen leads the body to increase the concentration of red blood cells in the blood so that more haemoglobin is available for oxygen transport. However the use of altitude training is much over rated, as there is no consistent evidence to show that performance improves upon return to sea level. Indeed in some cases performance is impaired. This may be due to poor training protocols at altitude, however. Here are some appropriate pointers.

Do not do strenuous training for a least two to three days until the stage of vulnerability to acute mountain sickness has passed.

Use a subjective method such as perceived exertion to determine the load in prolonged training sessions, rather than the stopwatch. Full workouts are not recommended until 7-10 days after arrival.

Lengthen the recovery periods in interval training. Remember that the resynthesis of ATP is an aerobic process and reduced oxygen availability means this process will take longer.

If possible, schedule intense sessions at lower altitudes.

Ensure that rehydration after training is adequate, as more fluids than normal may be lost during exercise in thin air.

There is an increased reliance on glycogen as a fuel for exercise at altitude so make sure you eat plenty of carbohydrates.

Competition at altitude is a different matter from the use of altitude training in an attempt to improve sea level performance. A period of acclimatisation is necessary for sports where oxygen uptake is a factor. In strength and sprint activities, though, no acclimatisation is necessary except to avoid altitude sickness.

10.10 The Effect of Smoking

Carbon monoxide, CO, which is present in cigarette smoke, has 300 times the affinity for haemoglobin, Hb, that oxygen has. This means that a fairly small concentration of CO can effectively tie up a substantial proportion of the blood's Hb thereby limiting the blood's oxygen carrying capacity and reducing Max VO_2. 10-12 cigarettes a day, depending on the type will tie up about 5% of the haemoglobin and 30-40 cigarettes per day can tie up almost 10% of the Hb. It may take a day or more of not smoking for the CO concentrations to return to normal. There are, of course, more damaging long-term effects of smoking that are well known.

STEPHEN WALKER

11 ADOPT & ADAPT

11.1 Staircases and Pyramids

So far I have outlined simple training methods based on every variation you can imagine between continuous activity and interval training with short work bouts and long rests. It should be clear to you now what is the purpose of each different method. It is possible to combine purposes within one training session by the use of pyramids where the quality and quantity of work bouts and rest periods vary in a structured way throughout the session.

For example you might wish to try to carry over some speed into your middle distance work. So a session could start with 5 x 10 sec sprints continue with 4 x 20 sec sprints then 3 x 40 sec, 2 x 1 min and 1 x 1 min 30 sec finishing with 1 x 2 min. On the other hand you may wish to practice a final sprint of a race when you are tired and so you tire yourself first with long intervals gradually reducing the duration whilst attempting to increase the speed. These are examples of staircases. Combine the two and you have what is referred to as a pyramid.

The scope for fitting interval training precisely to your requirements is enormous.

11.2 Circuit Training

Circuit training is generally arranged thus. A series of 10 - 15 exercises is laid out in a gym. First of all you go around each exercise for a test circuit in which you do as many repetitions of an exercise as possible in one minute. You record the result and move onto the next exercise after one minute of rest. At the next session you will have a card prepared showing your dose for each exercise. This dose is half the number of repetitions that you managed in your test. You then perform the circuit three times round against the clock, without rest. When you have got your circuit time down to three-quarters of your first attempt you retest yourself and get a new dose for future circuits.

The great thing about this sort of training is its specificity to you. You do your own individual training session that is adjusted to suit your ability. The drawback is that you first of all have to do a maximal test - not good without conditioning and especially if you are in any way fragile due to illness, injury or age.

There are other problems with this method. Clearly a 1-min. bout of activity places great demands on the lactic acid system. With only one minute of rest you quickly become exhausted and the number of repetitions possible in later exercises is not as great as it would have been, had you done them first. So when you come to do the circuit you find that the early exercises tax your ability considerably whereas the later exercise dosages seem inadequate.

The effect of circuit training seems to be that although you do not work at your maximum oxygen uptake your heart rate will be maximal and the feeling of stress will be high.

11.3 Alternative Circuit Training Regimens

Circuits with Set Doses

In this method the circuit can be laid out with a prepared dosage for each exercise. The dosage can even be graded in difficulty - easy, moderate, hard - and groups of people can still go round against the clock. The problem with group circuits tends to be the inevitable waiting at a particular station for a piece of essential apparatus to become free so that you can work at it.

Circuits with Set Work Periods

In this method everybody changes station at the same time so there is no waiting as above. Normally the work period is 25 seconds with 5 seconds allowed to get to the next exercise but simply shouting "Change!" every 30 seconds keeps everybody on the move and eliminates unwanted rest. The short work period means that the lactic acid system is not used much and if the exercise order is carefully chosen to use different muscle groups consecutively then continuous exercise may be performed. I have successfully managed large groups this way in relatively confined space with limited equipment using up to 30 different exercises with two or even three people to a station. It is in circumstances like this that the advantages of everybody changing station at once become apparent. It would be quite impossible for everybody to keep going continuously if they were allowed to go around the circuit at their own pace as frequent bottlenecks would lead inevitably to hold ups and enforced rest.

Circuit training need not always be arranged in such a way that exercise is continuous. Utilisation training does not really take place in circuit training even if the activity is continued for more than an hour. This is because, with the variety of exercises, muscles are being alternately worked and rested. Because the blood supply is always in the wrong muscle group the muscles have to work anaerobically. Circuits should therefore be intense and should not last longer than half an hour, in my humble opinion.

Interval Circuit Training

The training of the oxygen transport system can effectively be achieved with circuit training by, say, 4 x 4-min circuits with four minutes rest relief as opposed to continuous exercise. This pushes up the intensity and heart rate but allows for recovery. The exercises used should utilise large muscle groups so that large quantities of oxygen and blood must be pumped around the body by the heart. The exercises do not have to be the same in each consecutive circuit. Rest relief that is equal to the work period makes for easy organisation in groups. One group working whilst the other group is resting. Another way of organising an aerobic circuit is to spend, say, four minutes on each exercise. This ensures that the muscles fibres used are working aerobically. Care has to be taken here in the choice of exercise to make sure that it can be performed continuously for four minutes. This means that for the average person the load must be as low as 15% of their 1RM. Press-ups do not normally fall into this category, as I mentioned earlier.

Speed, Strength or Strength Endurance

For speed, strength or strength endurance plenty of rest needs to be included in the circuit after each exercise and the work bouts should be less than 30 seconds, preferably less than 15 seconds with rest periods of three times the work period. Going around the circuit in a group of three or four people with two or three resting and one at a time working leads to this result. The progress around the circuit could be arranged in two ways. Either the group does several sets of each exercise before moving on to the next exercise or else the group performs one set of each exercise before moving on, but they go round the circuit several times. If only for the sake of variety both methods should be used.

By keeping track of the number of repetitions executed in each exercise and the weight lifted (if a weight is used) a record of progress may be made.

Circuit Training the LA System

If tolerance to lactic acid in the body is sought then the work periods at each workstation should be longer, up to a minute or even two minutes with rest periods up to twice as long as the work periods. Groups of two or three people working at each single workstation will achieve this result. Clearly either light loads would have to be used or the exercises would have to the executed more slowly than for the short duration speed developing circuit.

11.4 Aerobics

Aerobics differs from most other types of training in that it is done to music. The suitability of the music has much to do with the quality of the workout. I have found aerobics to be amongst the hardest types of training I have ever done. On the other hand, I have attended classes that have brought me absolutely no benefit at all. So shop around for a class that suits your purpose in the light of the knowledge of exercise physiology that you have gained.

Most classes last for an hour but it is how the time is spent in this hour that determines what the effects upon your body will be. If the instructor allows you a rest at all then the effect will be quite different than if no rest is allowed. If the instructor concentrates on one muscle group for several exercises this will lead to a build up of lactic acid and local muscle fatigue which may force you to stop. This again is quite different to working on completely different muscle groups with each exercise, a technique which allows you to attack each exercise with more vigour and ultimately to use much more energy overall. Each method has its merits but you should be aware of what is happening and keep your ultimate sport objective at the back of your mind.

Matching exercises to the music is most important as it is impossible to perform all exercises at the same rhythm and it is important always to pick a pace that you find taxing. Inevitably as you improve you will find that a session may become too easy for you. If that becomes the case then you can impose an increased stress upon yourself by picking certain exercises to do double time (at twice the normal frequency).

The exercises themselves that are used in aerobics classes are many and various. Those exercises that use the largest and greatest number of muscle groups place the greatest demands on the oxygen system. Exercises involving small muscles or small numbers of muscles allow you to get your breath back and the heart rate to drop. Very strenuous exercises that cannot be performed continuously, if they are included in an aerobics session, should only be performed for very short periods, as otherwise strength endurance will be the limiting factor. The adequate supply of blood and oxygen to the muscles should be the limiting factor in aerobics.

Finally, it is worth noting that it is very difficult to exercise some muscle groups without apparatus. The biceps are a classic example.

11.5 Fartlek

Fartlek is a Scandinavian word meaning speed play. It was developed by runners and brought refreshing variety into training. Usually done over variable terrain and including jogging, walking, hill sprinting and continuous running it has been adopted and adapted for use in all sports. The effects very according to what is undertaken in the session and whilst it can turn out to be a very arduous training session it is all too easy for the quality of work to be inadequate for the provision of overload with no resultant improvement in performance. This has lead to "programmed fartlek" in which the session quality is controlled.

Low quality training sessions have their place in every training programme, though. Rest and recovery days are a vital ingredient in training, as vital as the work itself and genuine, go as you please fartlek, where you are under no pressure to perform, is a pleasant form of active restitution.

The typical example of a programmed fartlek training session might be:

Jog two miles
10 x 100m uphill sprints with walk downhill
Jog 800m
Walk 100m
One mile flat out
Jog 800m
Walk 100m
One mile flat out
Jog 800m
Walk 100m
2 x 6 exercise circuit with 10 repetitions of each exercise
Run two miles at moderate speed
15 flexibility exercises to finish off

12 PROGRAMMING TRAINING

Now that you have read all about the different training methods in use today and their effects you need to know how to piece them together in an optimal way for your sport.

12.1 In The Beginning

Start with low quality, low quantity aerobic training for initial conditioning. Use all the body in as many different ways as you can so as to build a broad base of condition upon which to mount your specific fitness. I covered this at the end of chapter 3 and you may find it worthwhile to review this section now.

12.2 Technique

In the year-round cycle of training you always have to set aside time for technique training. There are two major periods where this is emphasised. One is at the beginning of the off-season (if you have one in your sport) when training loads can be low, allowing more time for practising technique. The other is towards the final peak of the season, the major event. Because you are tapering off your training load to allow the body to recover completely from all the pressure to which you have subjected it, again you find yourself with time on your hands that can be devoted to practising and finally perfecting your technique.

This is necessarily a generalised remark. In some sports such as gymnastics or trick water skiing you perform far more work in practising your technique then you ever will in performing it at a competition. In other sports the work done in competition is as much if not greater than the work done in any training session. The latter case tends to be the ultra-endurance sports where fuelling up correctly plays a major part in success and good technique, which leads to efficiency, is developed over miles of training. Most other sports lie somewhere in between and, apart from the two special periods mentioned above, technique training continues throughout the year.

To perform with good technique you need to be fairly fresh. But to bring out your technical faults you sometimes need to be tired so practise in both conditions once you have mastered your skill.

12.3 Aerobic Fitness First

Even if your event places no demands on your oxygen system I recommend a period spent on training as opposed to conditioning your aerobic system before tackling strength training. Even with strength training the oxygen transport system has to supply oxygen after work to oxidise lactic acid and to re-generate ATP which will be needed to provide the energy for subsequent muscle contractions as well as to re-build torn tissue. Once you are on a full strength-training regime you can use low quality aerobic training sessions on rest days as active restitution.

12.4 Leave Anaerobic Glycolysis to the End

Lactic acid training is arduous and the psychological strain of it day after day takes its toll after a couple of months. So even if your major energy system is the lactic acid system do not train using it more than once or at most twice a week during the off season. Fortunately the benefits of training lactic acid system are quickly felt when you start on it. Remember that whilst it takes time and considerable effort to improve strength, speed and endurance these can be maintained by much less effort allowing you to devote more time to lactic acid training nearer your main event.

Furthermore if you start this type of training too early in the season you will run the risk of peaking too early, going stale or burning out later and subsequent peaking becomes much less predictable. If you have to perform well at two well separated events that require lactic acid training to reach a peak then revert to aerobic and/or strength training for a while after the first event. Remember that no event places demands solely on the lactic acid system so the other energy systems still need training.

12.5 Cyclic Training

Your training should proceed in cycles of overload alternating with recovery, the overload being progressively increased.

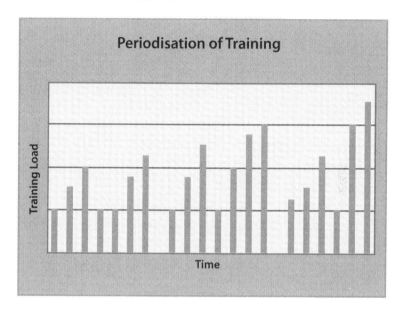

Figure 12.1

The columns shown in this example could represent days, weeks, months or even years of work at various training loads. If they represent days then these would be termed micro-cycles whereas if they were weeks or more then they would be termed macro-cycles.

On a daily basis no more than 3 heavy training days in succession can be tolerated because of glycogen depletion. This would only be undertaken towards the end of the season in any case as it takes time to build up to this. At the beginning of the season probably every hard day is followed by an easier day. In the middle of the season two hard days followed by one light day would be suitable.

Macro-cycles

Macrocycles are usually either two weekly, three weekly or four weekly cycles ending in a competition or some sort of a test or trial.

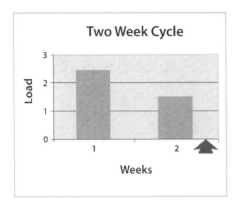

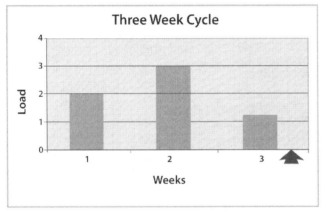

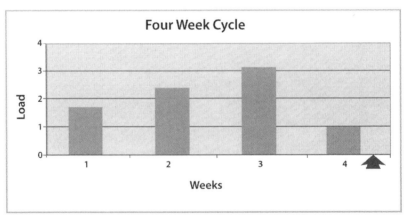

Figure 12.2

In the rough guidelines represented by these diagrams load could represent km of training or tonnes of weight lifted, for example. Each diagram shows an easy week before the competition, marked by an arrow thus, 🔺. It is plain that the four-week cycle represents the greatest overall load. In the four-week cycle only one week in four is light whereas in the two-week cycle every other week is light.

The Danes and Norwegians one-year had different methods of selection for their national rowing teams. The Norwegians were selected early whereas the Danes had to prove themselves at a series of trials throughout the season. This meant that the Danes had to keep tapering off their training so as to be able to perform well in the trials if they wanted selection. Meanwhile the Norwegians were able to keep training hard without much interruption. The maximum oxygen uptake of the Danes at the beginning of the season was higher than that of the Norwegians but by the end of the season the positions had reversed. The Danish coaches were able to show to the selectors that max VO_2 was proportional to the intensity of the training and as a result were able to get the selection procedure altered for future years. The two or three week training cycle that the Danes had been obliged to use did not afford adequate intensity, as a four-week cycle would have done.

Bear in mind with this example that rowing training for 2,000m, which takes between 5 1/2 minutes and 8 1/2 minutes at international level, depending upon boat type, involves training over much greater distances than are endured in racing. Contrast this to the marathon racer who cannot realistically train, day after day, over distances substantially longer than a marathon (even though such feats have been achieved) because of a lack of time to work for a living amongst other things. For most marathoners the event itself represents the greatest training load that can be expected in a day in terms of both quality and quantity so racing forms an important part of training whereas for many other sports people the competition day is like a day off. The point I am trying to make here is that in designing a training program you have to take into account whether a competition represents an increase or a decrease in the training load in your assessment of the overall intensity of the training program. If it represents an increase then more frequent competition will not necessarily be a bad thing. In fact it may be ideal training. If on the other hand it represents a decrease then you may have to avoid frequent competition in order to gain sufficient long-term improvement for the most important competition.

Micro-cycles

These are usually arranged on a weekly basis, for obvious reasons, with training peaks usually occurring at weekends, when most people have more leisure time. An example of the three-week cycle ending in a standard pre-race week is shown here. The load represented by competition varies according to the sport, the level of competition encountered, whether you have a lot of rounds of competition to get through and so on. It can be unpredictable and account must be taken of the competition in deciding upon the training (or resting) that follows.

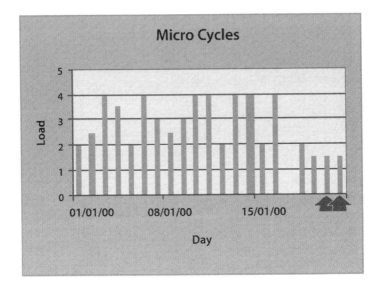

Figure 12.3

It is most important during the final approach to a big event to allow complete recovery from training. This has to be balanced against the risk of de-training, that is, losing the benefits gained in training by subsequent inactivity. However, after prolonged and arduous training the risk of losing the benefits are low. Of course, if you have not been training hard then you cannot taper off. If you have been training hard then you can still reap the benefits after several weeks of inactivity.

12.6 Overtraining - Under-recovery

The motivation of athletes to train hard can sometimes be a handicap instead of an asset. If you do not allow sufficient time for recovery with an adequate diet and rest then you run the risk of not being ready for your next training session. The micro and macro cycles shown above include light days to permit the essential recovery of the body so that improved performance may ensue. This was covered earlier in the overload principle.

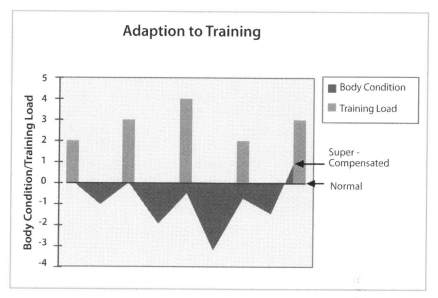

Figure 12.4

This is a schematic diagram showing the body's recuperation to above normal fitness levels when it is allowed to recover.

Now imagine the result if no recovery is allowed. The body's condition deteriorates steadily and no improvement in performance is possible.

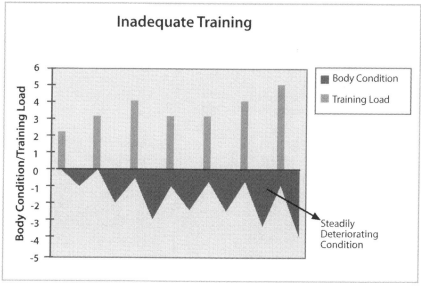

Figure 12.5

Now in this condition training performances deteriorate and you begin to think that you are losing form because you are not training hard enough. So instead of resting you put in extra training sessions! You suffer from sleeplessness and loss of appetite in this condition when what you need is more sleep and more food to replenish your glycogen depots. You probably also become irritable. At this stage you may also display symptoms of hypoglycaemia where low levels of blood sugar begin to affect the central nervous system which relies on blood sugar for its operation. These symptoms are dizziness, partial blackout, nausea and confusion. All you need is to stop training and eat properly for a few days and then to revise your training program so that it includes adequate recovery time. After an experience like this you should become more sensitive to your condition and instead of taking poor training times as a signal to train harder you should take them as a warning that a rest is overdue.

When I was 16 I ran a mile in 4 minutes 47.6 seconds. The following year I could not get under 4.55 no matter what I did. So I trained harder. When I finished my last school examinations I virtually spend my whole days training. Intervals, longer runs, sprinting, anything. You name it, I did it but I did not go any faster. Then I took on a vacation job, which prevented me from training because of shift work. After two weeks of barely training at all I attended an athletics meeting and knocked three seconds of my half-mile time. In the same meeting I then ran a mile in 4.40. This was a 15-second improvement over my best that year! I was delighted. Another month went by with hardly any training at all and I attended a one-mile time trial at my club. Imagine my astonishment when after six weeks of minimal training I managed a time of 4.33. This was almost 22 seconds faster than I had run whilst I was in training that year.

I had fallen into the overtraining trap I described earlier and I had not been allowing my body to recover. So, of course, my times were poor until I did allow it to recover. This is why I said earlier that the risk of losing the benefits of hard training during a tapering off period is low. This experience of mine as a teenager was one of the most astounding lessons I ever learned but it was many years before I acquired sufficient knowledge to understand it.

A more recent and startling example was El Gerrouj's world record in the mile at Rome. He had been out of competition for four or five weeks owing to injury yet when he returned he ran an incredible 3 minutes 43.13 seconds! I know it rather puts my teenage performance into perspective but it proves the point I am trying to make about layoffs not mattering too much provided you have done the training in the first place.

12.7 Different Recovery Rates

Unfortunately there are no hard and fast rules regarding recovery rates. Some people recover from training exceptionally quickly whilst others recover exceptionally slowly. At low frequencies of training, especially at moderate intensities it does not matter greatly but as you become better and keener and you train harder and with greater frequency you may easily reach the point at which no improvement is possible.

Arthur Jones, founder of Nautilus, has shown that with exceptionally intense strength training the frequency of training is best reduced from three sessions per week to a mere two sessions so that adequate recovery can take place and greater loads lifted at each successive training session. Lifting greater loads in strength training is the name of the game, after all.

As each individual's ability to recover is different it is important that you monitor carefully your own subjective feelings about your condition so that you can nip overtraining in the bud. The training diary is most helpful in this respect and I recommend that you record much more information than the training that you have done. You should record your competition performances, the weather conditions, what you have been eating, your resting heart rate and how you feel and a possible explanation for why you feel that way.

Measuring your heart rate each morning when you get up is useful in assessing how well recovered your body is. Provided that you are not woken by an alarm your heart rate will probably be lowest whilst you are still in bed. However, almost any attempt to measure it will involve movement and then it will change. A good protocol to adopt is to take your pulse while sitting down after first emptying your bladder. If your heart rate is 10 beats higher than normal then you are either incompletely recovered or you are ill. Either way you should not train. If your heart rate is 5 beats higher than normal you should consider having a light day or a recovery day.

12.8 Speed Work

As I remarked earlier, marathon running is quite different to 100m sprinting even though they are both running events. The difference in action at different speeds is apparent in all sports and because different muscles are used in different ranges of movement, in the name of specificity, you must train these different muscles after prolonged endurance work before attempting to go fast over moderate distances. If, for example, you have been cycling 100 miles a day to build up your endurance and raise your anaerobic threshold but you are ultimately aiming at a five mile time trial, which you expect to cover in 10 minutes, then you need to do some max VO_2 training over, say, 2, 3 and 4 minute intervals. But in order to go fast enough to do some real good you first need to train those, so far, unused muscles by doing some really short bursts of near flat out speed training. The technique will be quite different but you will go faster in your subsequent interval training and that will enable you to improve your longer distance racing.

The occasional speed session will then maintain your form for the lactic acid training you must do throughout your season. At the end of the season, when you lay off lactic acid training to allow for recovery before the "big championship", you can use your sprint training to put a final razor sharp peak on top of all that form without taxing yourself unduly.

12.9 Summary

Start with the aerobic conditioning and follow with aerobic training, no matter what your ultimate ambition.

Work from broadly based general all round training with considerable variety through activities directly related to your sport towards the specific activity itself.

Break down your sport into its component parts and train them separately. This means the separate muscle groups, the separate skills and the individual energy systems.

Remember that whenever you overload a particular aspect there is a trade-off in specificity. This means, for example, that you must train at speeds above and below that required in competition. Tempo training is an essential part of tapering.

If the lactic acid system predominates in your sport remember that it does not ever provide 100% of the required energy and so train the other energy system or systems first leaving the psychologically taxing lactic acid training to the end of your programme. Speed work may be included for variety during the "endurance" training.

Do not overtrain. In both strength and endurance programmes it is easy for fatigue to creep up on you and trick you into doing more training when you should do less. With lactic acid training, fatigue does not creep up; it leaps up on you!

Take the intensity of competition into account when you plan your programme.

Practise technique all year round but especially at the end of the off season whilst you are getting back into condition and again when you taper for the big event.

13 TESTS ON TRIAL

The ultimate test is the ultimate competition and if the outcome of that competition could be predicted by physiological or psychological tests then we might as well all test ourselves on machines and select the world champion by posting the results to each other without any competition at all! Since I originally wrote this sentence this has come to pass. Concept II has a worldwide pecking order for performances on their rowing ergometers and these results have become a virtual competition. Actual face to face, side by side competition does take place on these machines as well, it has to be said.

13.1   Strength Testing
13.2   Testing Anaerobic Power
13.3   Skill in Tests
13.4   What can be established by Testing?
13.5   Submaximal Tests
13.6   Conclusion

13.1 Strength Testing

Strength training is strength testing and you will inevitably be able to assess your level of strength and its progress simply by keeping records of your training. To increase strength you have to put your muscles under maximal stress and in so doing you find out the limit of your strength.

If you find yourself getting weaker as a consequence of strength training then you are not allowing yourself to recover adequately before testing your strength. The immediate effect of training is a reduction in your performance capacity whereas the ultimate result of training is an improvement. But you have to wait for this result and some people take substantially longer to recover than others, so do not be surprised to find that whilst your training partner has recovered you have not.

Remember

STEPHEN WALKER

Remember too that for most people the results of strength training are specific to the muscle exercised and even more specifically to the range of movement that is stressed most in that exercise. I say for most people because there are some people whose muscle strength improves over the whole range when only part of the range is stressed.

13.2 Testing Anaerobic Power

Power is rate of work or work per unit time. Work is force times distance moved in the direction of the applied force.

Therefore:

Power = Force x distance/time = Force x velocity

$$P = F \times d / t$$

When assessing anaerobic power the often overlooked factor is the athlete's own body weight, or in the case of rotational movement, such as discus or hammer throwing, the athlete's own moment of inertia. The athlete's weight or moment of inertia has to be moved and if this is not correctly accounted for in the measurement then the absolute power may not be measured. Take, for example, the use of the Sergeant Jump as a means are measuring anaerobic power. The comparison of one individual's maximum jump height over their maximum reach is not a direct comparison of anaerobic power since clearly the 100 kg athlete who jumps vertically 0.5 m produces more power than the 70 kg athlete who jumps the same height.

Quite frankly I can see little value in knowing your anaerobic power as a result of a test of this nature. Of course, if there were a high correlation between a high anaerobic power as measured by the test and a high degree of success in your particular sport then the test would be relevant. Often such tests are conducted simply in order to establish that there is or is not such a correlation. The results of these tests cannot therefore benefit you in anyway as they are designed to accumulate knowledge and understanding that will benefit future generations of athletes.

13.3 Skill in Tests

A height degree of skill in the execution of a test exercise will inevitably lead to a better performance. So it is neither fair nor possible to compare one athlete with another or with a predetermined standard or norm using a battery of test exercises such as those found in a circuit test. It simply is not possible to control accurately the execution of a movement such as a dip on the parallel bars or a squat thrust so that one person is doing the same amount of work per repetition as another. Clearly body weight affects the amount of work done but body dimensions can affect the efficiency of the movement

160

also. Short-legged people, for example, generally find squat trusts easier than longer legged people do. Some people have heavy legs and light trunks whereas others are built the opposite way around. The former would find sit-ups easier than leg-raises whereas the latter would find the opposite and either exercise might falsely be considered to be a measure of stomach muscle fitness. You begin to see how difficult it is to devise meaningful tests.

13.4 What can be established by Testing?

My experience of batteries of tests with groups of trainees is that the exceptionally good and the exceptionally bad athletes always stand out quite obviously. Those in the middle, though, are difficult to separate with any degree of meaningful accuracy and their skill in their chosen sport would ultimately determine their position in the pecking order. This, of course, can only be tested in the specific sport itself, not by a "test".

An athlete's potential is virtually impossible to assess in one test because the state of training cannot be established. However, the same test or tests conducted over some weeks, months or years will reveal the state of training because the untrained will improve faster than the pre-trained. It is this measure of progress that is the most useful aspect of tests in my view. An example of this is shown below.

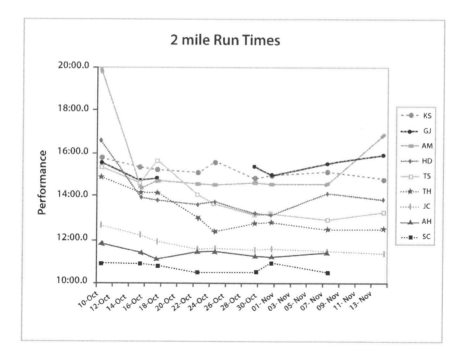

Figure13.1

This shows the time achieved for a 2 mile run by various individuals within the same training group over a two-month period. The run was always done after circuit training.

As training and fitness improved, as expected, the time taken to do the run fell progressively. Generally speaking the least fit improved the fastest initially with everybody eventually reaching a point at which improvement became gradual or erratic.

However the results of this test do require some interpretation. TS and TH showed the typical improvement one might expect from young poorly trained athletes.

AM was a young highly trained swimmer who initially ran slowly because of unfamiliarity with running but once he had found his best pace he was quite unable to improve upon it.

JC was a quite naturally gifted runner in his mid '20s and showed a significant improvement until he got close to his maximum performance.

All the other athletes shared irregularities in performance which might not have been expected but which are readily explained.

GJ was improving until she got a back injury, which forced her to layoff running. This was followed by flu and an extension to the lay off. The next run was, not surprisingly, poor. There was a significant improvement but then a relapse into illness. Again upon return to training, performance was poor as might have been expected.

HD was showing a steady improvement but gave blood around 5th November just before her penultimate performance. Although the blood volume may be replenished fairly quickly the manufacture of oxygen carrying erythrocytes takes much longer, weeks if not months, and performance is impaired.

AH was a veteran with many years of training behind him so the consistent times were to be expected. However the exceptionally good time on 17th October needs to be accounted for. This, fortunately, is quite simple, as he did not do the circuit training beforehand on this occasion.

SC was another veteran, likewise with many years training experience. The deterioration on 31st October was due to his imbibing three glasses of wine at an office party only 30 minutes before starting the evening training.

Almost all the athletes showed a marked improvement in their performance when a handicap system was introduced on 24th October. This illustrates the importance of motivation in performance and demonstrates the difficulty of providing controlled conditions for a maximal test.

The variability of the performances shows how foolhardy it would be to judge an athlete on the basis of one test on one occasion.

It is important to understand what a test of this nature is actually measuring. A 2-mile run is substantially aerobic so aerobic work capacity is a major limiting factor. You should understand, however, that in running the athlete's body weight is continually lifted up and down and that the run time reflects the aerobic power to weight ratio which is measured in ml oxygen per kg of body weight per minute, ml kg^{-1} min^{-1} or ml/kg/min. If you are engaged in a sport where the absolute measure of aerobic power, the maximum oxygen uptake in litres per minute (which is independent of body weight) is of greater significance then you should divide the run times by each athlete's weight before making any comparison between athletes. For example a time of 13 minutes achieved by a 100kg athlete yields a lower figure, 0.13, than a time of 11 minutes achieved by a 70kg athlete, 0.157. Therefore the 100kg athlete has a greater maximal aerobic power than the 70kg athlete despite having a poorer run time. This can be very encouraging to heavy people who might otherwise feel inferior to their lightweight counterparts when running.

13.5 Submaximal Tests

The run described above whilst actually part of training, nevertheless acts as a maximal test also. There are a number of tests, which can be performed at submaximal levels, leading to predictions of maximal aerobic power or some other figure that may be compared with statistical norms. Again my experience with these tests is that there are few surprises and the outstanding athletes, good or bad, show up clearly. The value of them is that they do not require maximal efforts and are therefore useful in testing subjects who are not trained or who may be medically unfit. Submaximal tests also enable you to detect improvements in your fitness without having to produce a maximal effort, something you should only have to do in an important competition. Furthermore, a submaximal test can indicate to you that you are either ill or not fully recovered without doing to you the sort of serious harm that a maximal effort might do.

The tests all rely upon the well established principal that heart rate, HR, is related directly to work load and oxygen uptake and that there is a limit to the maximum heart rate and therefore to maximal aerobic power. The heart is best monitored during the work period, which must last at least 3 minutes for a steady physiological state to be reached. However some tests allow for measurement of heart rates after the work period. For this to be accurate there must be a good correlation between HR during work and the HR after work. This is unfortunately not strictly the case so the accuracy of the result is always suspect. However, they do give a rough guide and maybe useful in some circumstances.

The tests can involve any aerobic activity. Most data has been collected on cycle ergometers or treadmills but rowing or canoeing ergometers can be used, even stepping up and down on a bench. It is important to bear in mind always that aerobic power is activity specific. Most people cannot achieve the same oxygen uptake with their arms as they can with their legs, for example. However, canoeists can! Get the point? It is one thing to draw conclusions about an individual runner's potential from an aerobic power test conducted on a treadmill. It is quite another to predict the swimming potential of a canoeist from an aerobic test run on a treadmill. Be careful about the conclusions that you draw from a test.

13.6 Step Tests

The two most well known step tests are the Harvard Step Test, developed in 1942 as a screening test for the armed services, and the Astrand Rhyming step test. Both involve stepping up and down 30 times a minute for 5 minutes. The principle is that a steady state of energy expenditure is reached and the level of stress can be determined from the heart rate at the end of the exercise period. The body weight is lifted through a known distance (the height of the bench) at a known rate so the power output per unit body weight is the same for everybody. Power output is directly related to oxygen uptake, which is directly related to heart rate (HR) for any individual. Maximum HR is approximately 220 minus age i.e. 190 for a 30 year old or 205 for a 15 year old. So if we know the HR at a given power output and we know the maximum HR we can estimate the maximum power output and the maximum oxygen uptake (for stepping).

There are a number of sources of error in this method.

Whilst the linear increase in HR with oxygen uptake is a typical feature there are many exceptions. For example some people can show an increase in their oxygen uptake at their maximum HR with no increase in their HR. The maximum oxygen uptake for such people would therefore be underestimated by an extrapolation from the HR response to submaximal loads.

Although I. Astrand gave us a means of correcting for age, her system assumes a given maximum HR for a given age. But the standard deviation for maximal HR within an age group is plus or minus ten beats per minute and this will clearly affect the accuracy of the predictions.

Without HR monitoring equipment the usual procedure is to take the pulse after exercise. Indeed the standard Harvard Step Test requires that the pulse be measured between 1 and 1.5 minutes, 2 and 2.5 minutes and between 3 and 3.5 minutes after exercise. The correlation between HR during exercise and HR after exercise has been shown to be reasonable for an individual but poor for a group because we all recover at different rates. This means that recovery HR gives only a rough idea of the HR attained during work if the results are compiled from different subjects and this makes comparison of the result of one individual's test with another less meaningful. The comparison of one individual's test with a previous result does however give a meaningful indication of improvement or deterioration in fitness.

If the test is used then account has to be taken of any differences in bench height from that in the test specification, and variation in the rate of stepping.

If an absolute power evaluation is required then the weight of the athlete must be included in the calculation.

Even when all this has been done, one can still come across the unusual or unpredictable result. Take this example.

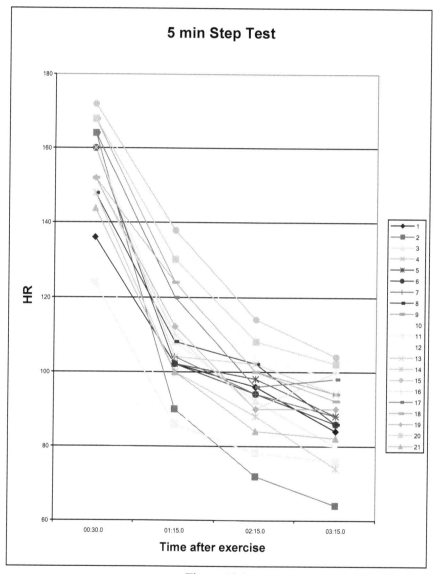

Figure 13.2

The points represent the HR for 21 individuals after a 5-minute step test on a 51cm bench. Subject 11 is AH from figure 13.1 whom we can tell is quite fit by looking at his run time. Subject 12 represents a large and very fit oarsman/rugby player whose Max VO_2 I have more than once estimated to be over 5 litres per minute. Subject 14 represents a talented female. As might be expected these curves are all near the bottom of the group of curves shown.

However subject 15 represents a very fit female who was the fastest runner of all the females in the group. So why are the points representing her HR right at the top of the group? Well she was HD in fig 13.1 and it was she who gave blood a few days before the step test. Obviously she had a smaller oxygen carrying capacity and this was why her heart had to beat so fast.

If we assume her weight to be approximately 58kg and that women typically have a blood volume of 65ml per kg then her blood volume would normally be 3.7 litres. So, giving say, 0.5 litres of blood represents a 13.5% reduction in the oxygen carrying capacity of her blood. From this we can estimate that without giving blood her HR after the test would have been 152 instead of 172. This would have been much nearer the expected figure.

13.7 Conclusions

Submaximal tests are inaccurate predictors of maximal aerobic power but maximal tests are dangerous for the medically unfit. Tests need to be relevant to your sport, as even your maximum oxygen uptake will differ according to the test activity used to measure it. A single test is fairly meaningless because it reveals nothing about your potential for improvement and takes no account of special circumstances that may lead to an untypical result.

Submaximal tests using a heart rate monitor are to be preferred over tests that rely upon heart rate measured after exercise. Carefully designed submaximal tests making use of appropriate equipment can help you to discover whether you are fit or unwell without the need to perform the sort of effort that should be reserved for important competitions.

Strength testing is largely unnecessary as strength training itself usually gives clear indications of improvement.

The capacity of the lactic acid system is virtually impossible to assess, as it is not possible to separate the points at which one energy system takes over from another.

More information exists on aerobic capacity than on any other measure of fitness. But there are many pitfalls in the measurement of maximum oxygen uptake, the accurate assessment of which I have not covered here. Self assessment from simple tests involving the monitoring of the HR response to standardised loads is most meaningful if carried out on a number of occasions thereby revealing your progress in training. Do not place too much emphasis on test results. The Italians once tested over 900 rowers on ergometers yet none of the best scorers were in the medal winning crews at the world championships!

14 MIND YOUR HEAD

At the top level in sports it is almost impossible to do any more training as the athletes simply do not have sufficient hours in a week to eat and sleep as well as train and, most importantly, recover. This begs the question "Do professional athletes perform better because they have more time to train or because they have more time to recover?"

They are all extremely talented and have very similar physiological characteristics. Tuning for big events is fairly well understood and competitors arrive in a similar state of readiness. Their will to win is undoubted, so what separates them on the day? At the very top-level the differences are largely psychological. To be psychologically prepared and in the right condition to win is sometimes your only advantage. To be able to out-psych your opponent. To be able to make rational tactical decisions that are correct. Here experience can be your friend. But past experiences can also work against you unwittingly because of the power of your subconscious mind. But if you can train and harness that power, then.......

This power of the subconscious is so great that a lesser man can beat a world champion. But the supreme mental effort required to do this is difficult to reproduce. You may not remember who beat Boris Becker at Wimbledon in 1987. I am unable to find it out but I remember it. Whoever he was, on that day he excelled himself. In beating Becker he achieved the impossible. But in the next round he was a shadow by comparison. Psychologically he was a spent force. That supreme effort had taken its toll.

In this chapter I will explain how to tap this great resource so that you can win when you really want to. But first let us look at some basic ground rules

14.1 Performance and Arousal Levels

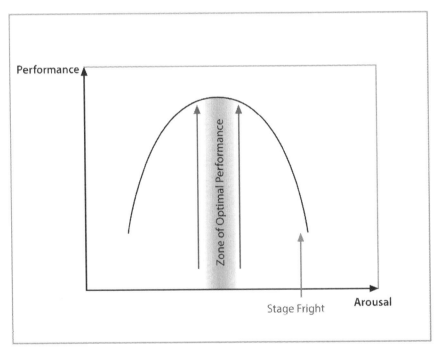

Figure 14.1

Figure 14.1 shows the, now widely accepted, inverted U shape of the performance/arousal curve. Arousal can be taken to mean excitement, anxiety, pressure or stress. It probably has a lot to do with the amount of adrenaline circulating in the body. At low arousal levels motivation is low and performance is a struggle. The stimulus of competition, even against a training partner may be enough to raise your performance substantially and with luck the cheering and support of club mates or spectators at an important event may induce just the right level arousal to elicit a peak performance.

On the other hand your average performance may already be good. Competition with a training partner may be better or even optimal and competition at major events may take you over the top of the curve and down the other side so that you feel over stressed and do not perform at your best.

Two individuals who spring to my mind as typical examples of this are David Bedford, the British 10,000m runner and Ron Clarke the Australian middle distance runner. Both were prolific record breakers, Ron Clarke in particular, but neither seemed able to pull off the important gold medal winning performance. It was as though the big occasion, such as the Olympics, simply put them under too much stress. They went over the top of the inverted U and down the other side! Indeed so many people "drop their shopping" at the Olympics that it is often unnecessary to produce a personal best performance in order to win the gold medal.

14.2 Task Complexity

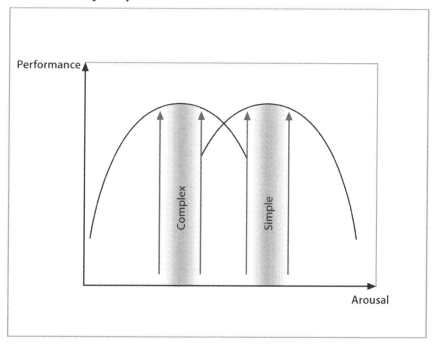

Figure 14.2

Figure 14.2 shows that the optimal arousal level is higher for a simple task such as running than it is for a complex task such as playing tennis. Put another way, you have to control your arousal level, remaining cool, calm and collected in a stressful situation in order to play your optimum game of tennis.

14.3 Factors Affecting Arousal

There are great many factors that can affect your arousal level and take you towards or away from your optimal arousal level. The classic one is the effect of the crowd. Spectators or supporters can sense a close competition or the chance of a record and vociferous support can lift an athlete to new levels of performance. I saw this recently. The extremely loud cheering from a large club in support of one of its members, who had to all intents and purposes already lost the race he was in, revitalised him and he stormed towards the finish like a new man, to be beaten, as it turned out, by just one foot.

On the other hand noise can be very distracting in situations where great accuracy and concentration are required such as in tennis, golf, snooker, dressage and shooting. Supporters of such sports are usually conscious of this and are therefore well behaved or well controlled but the noise of a passing motorcycle or somebody dropping something accidentally can be all that is necessary to distract a competitor. It is therefore important in training to teach yourself to become bomb proof. I once knew a modern pentathlon coach who used to throw Ping-Pong balls at his athletes when they were shooting so that they learned to shut out the rest of the world and concentrate on the task at hand.

Stress or fright can elicit higher than normal performance. Ikai and Steinhaus (1961) found that firing a 22-caliber gun between 2 and 10 seconds before a subject was asked to give a maximal arm flexion had the effect of increasing performance. [They fired blanks and no athlete was harmed in the study!] Shouting, hypnosis, adrenaline and amphetamine also tended to improve performance. Interestingly the effects were most pronounced in untrained subjects, the implication being that the limit to muscular contraction is some in-built inhibition which training has already disinhibited in the trained athlete.

The presence or absence of a loved one or a coach can dramatically affect arousal in a positive or a negative way. Stress induced by the attention of the media at a big event can raise arousal levels to the point where you become ineffective in competition. A swimmer succumbed to this pressure at the Olympics in 1984 and ended up overtraining instead of relaxing. He finished fourth, having been tipped to win. He subsequently went on to win the event in 1988 by a mere 1/100th of the second!

14.4 Symptoms of Stress

It is all very well knowing that all these factors (and many more I have not mentioned) can affect your arousal level and cause you to win or lose an important medal. What you need to know, though, is what your optimal level of arousal is and how to achieve it so that you can win when you most desire to win. Desire to win is an important factor too. If you are not excited about the prospect of winning, if you could not really care less whether or not you win then you are much less likely to win. But I digress. First of all, let us consider some of the symptoms of stress and excitement that can give you some feedback about your level of arousal. These symptoms are the same for world-class athletes as they are for club level athletes. The only major differences between them is that because of their natural talent world-class athletes have to travel farther afield to meet the sort of competition that is going to provide them with the same satisfaction that club athletes can get competing locally.

Collywobbles are the most obvious sign. The feeling that your stomach has just turned over or that a butterfly is fluttering about inside you. Often experienced on the journey to an event when you have little else to do but sit and think about it. But thinking about the event weeks or even months before can make your stomach turn over. Collywobbles are quite normal and not a matter for concern. In fact I would say that as an indication of a first step up the arousal ladder collywobbles are probably a good thing in the vast majority of cases.

Nervous bladder and bowels. Again it is commonplace to find competitors making frequent visits to the loo, sometimes with little or no result. On one important day I seemed to spend every spare moment on the toilet but I won my event nevertheless. A very severe fright can leave you with brown trousers but such frights are more common in war than in sport.

A pounding heart is a typical response to stress. If you are in a quiet situation you may feel it suddenly start to boom as adrenaline pumps into your bloodstream from the adrenal medulla. If you monitor your heart rate you will doubtless be aware that during competition day your HR is elevated. That day I spent on the lavatory my HR never dropped below 100 even though I was fully recovered between each heat. The adrenaline kept my HR up. It has been established that HR is elevated even before exercise is undertaken. We normally associate HR elevation with the response to exercise and indeed the heart does respond to exercise. But in anticipation of exercise the presence of the hormone, adrenaline, has the effect of raising HR, increasing the force of contraction of the heart and thereby increasing cardiac output. Adrenaline has other beneficial effects.

- Raising the mean arterial blood pressure
- Reducing the resistance to blood flow by dilating arteries in the muscles

- Increasing the amount of available blood sugar
- Mobilising free fatty acids
- Stimulating the central nervous system making the passage of nerve impulses quicker and easier.

Nausea and vomiting are less common symptoms of nervous stress in my experience but they can nevertheless stem from nerves and indicate a high arousal level. Whether you need this level of stress to elicit that world beating performance or whether such nervousness is counterproductive can only be established by experience. Often the nausea will disappear once you start your competition and will not reappear between heats. Self-confidence is a big factor here. Once you find yourself coping with the situation the stress is reduced. Experience of competition will reduce the likelihood of nausea. However, a tendency to suffer from nausea may return when competing at a higher level that has not previously been encountered.

Other indicators of stress are sweaty palms and sweating under the armpits but these are more often associated with the stress of an interview than with physical performance.

Sleeplessness also often accompanies stress or excitement and I have seen it recommended that you persuade a doctor to prescribe a mild sleeping tablet in the run up to an important competition. However, the tablet should not be taken the night before competition in case drowsiness persists into the competition day but it should be used on the night previous to that to ensure a good night's sleep and aid full recovery from training. A poor night's sleep immediately prior to competition has not been shown to impair performance though of course this would be extremely difficult to prove. I myself have never resorted to sleeping tablets but then with a lifetime of competition under my belt I have never found that the prospect of competition has made me sufficiently nervous to warrant their use.

Irritability, snappiness and short temper often accompany stress before competition. It is as well to be aware that somebody may be in the firing line in these circumstances, a team-mate upon whom you might depend or your coach or partner.

You may become quiet in your contemplation of the event and find conversation tiresome. The attention of the press or family can prove disruptive at such times and you are best taking yourself away to a quiet place if you can. Many seasoned competitors, aware of this, will not arrive at the Olympic Village, say, until just prior to their event.

14.5 Extroversion and Arousal

We all have natural levels of arousal determined by our characters and personalities. The way we are made up determines how far up the performance arousal curve we are naturally. It has been shown that extroverts have a lower natural arousal level than do introverts. An attention-seeking extrovert needs more encouragement in order to reach his/her optimal performance level than does the quiet introvert for whom too much attention could be disadvantageous. A coach who understands this will not treat all members of a team in the same way, possibly choosing to take the introvert aside for some quiet advice whilst criticising the extrovert publicly in front of his team mates.

Interestingly also, it has been shown that on a treadmill provided with a chicken button introverts will generally chicken out when the heart rates reach 130 beats per minute whilst extroverts will not press the button until 160 beats per minute.

However, introverts have a high conditionability being content with the same old dose day after day whilst the low conditionability of extroverts means that doses must be varied in order to prevent boredom and maintain stimulus.

14.6 Controlling Arousal

Herein lies the secret of success. When you have done all the physical training that is necessary, when your equipment is just right, you have allowed just the right time for recovery, you feel good and you feel it is your turn to get lucky, when you know you are invincible then the only thing you have left to do is to get your arousal level just right. You have to get yourself in the zone of optimal performance. If you perfect this, nothing will bother you, nothing will deflect you from your task, all your physical and mental effort will be directed towards the objective, winning, and you will win.

I remember feeling this way at competition once. It was my turn to win, I was convinced. I had won my heat in a time of 4.03. Looking at the times for the other two heats I could see that one of them had also been won in the same time, 4.03. I had been in a close race but the other competitor had not be pressed, which indicated that perhaps he had more in reserve that I had. It did not help to know that he was an ex-Italian lightweight international. However, I still felt it was going to be my turn. But I was nervous. I could feel the arousal level getting higher and higher as the day went by. Eventually I knew I was boiling over and if I did not do something I might fluff it. So I took myself away to a dark part of a restaurant at the event, sat down, put my feet up and my head back and shut my eyes. I must have been there for between half and three quarters of an hour. Some club mates came in and joked about my being asleep. But I was not asleep. I was psyching myself down - not psyching myself up, but down. I went over the race to come, in my head, again and again. I practised my start in my head. I covered every eventuality: being behind, being ahead, being level, having a minor upset, making a tactical era, everything going right, the effect of a gust of wind, the rhythm of my movements, the shouting of supporters, the warning of an umpire; until I was calm and totally in control. My heart was no longer racing out of control. It was in control. Then I went out and did some limbering up before going to the start. From the word "GO!" I was ahead and I just kept going ahead until I won. And the time was 3.53, a whole ten seconds faster than the heat when I had thought I had gone as fast as I could.

Unwittingly, I had done several things right in my psychological preparation. Firstly, I had found a quiet place to go where sounds would not distract me unduly. Secondly, it was also fairly dark so that with my eyes shut I had no visual distractions. Thirdly, by putting my feet up and my head back I was able to relax. Fourthly, in this relaxed position I lowered my level of consciousness, not to the point where I fell asleep, but low enough so that I could gain access to my subconscious and implant therein the image of success.

14.7 Feedback of Heart Rate

I mentioned here that my heart had been a racing out of control. This factor is tied into the feeling of boiling over and becoming over-aroused caused largely by adrenaline. However, you can use your heart rate to control your arousal instead of the other way around, simply by closing the feedback loop. Give yourself information about your heart rate and immediately you will find that you can control it to some extent. I have found it particularly helpful to monitor my heart rate on my temple so that I almost hear it as well as feel it and the effect on my brain and my arousal level is more immediate.

The time interval between any two heart-beats is never the same. In other words the heart rate is continually changing. This is known as heart rate variability, HRV. HR is affected by breathing rate and by the body's own temperature regulation mechanism in a cyclic way and you will find that by controlling your breathing you can control your HR to some extent. You will find that monitoring your HR regularly will provide you with another tool to help monitor and control your arousal.

14.8 Your Subconscious Computer

In your everyday activities you make thousands of decisions without even thinking about what you are doing. They are not conscious decisions and you are not aware that you are making them. When you say, "my car knows its own way to work" you reveal that your subconscious computer has taken over the everyday task of driving your car and that no conscious thought is required. Only in a motoring crisis where conscious decisions have to be made to, say, avoid an accident will the subconscious relinquish control to the conscious. At such a moment you will probably find that if you were listening to the radio you might miss an important item of news that you wanted to hear.

Your subconscious computer makes many decisions for you even in such a simple task as scratching your forehead; which finger or fingers of which hand to use, whether to scratch or rub, lightly or vigorously, whether to put down first something that you are holding before scratching, which muscles to engage and in what order. The amount of information handled in this simple task and the number of decisions taken at incredible speed remind one of the complexity of the calculations necessary to achieve a rendezvous in space. Space agencies use computers costing millions to arrange for the meeting of spacecraft in outer space and yet our tiny brains can perform tasks which to us appear simple but would be impossible to program into a computer. Tasks such as riding a bicycle through a crowded street or washing dishes, drying them and putting them away. What is so amazing is that so much can be done without thought, that is, subconsciously. Your subconscious computer is the most astounding resource and the secret of success is to gain access to it and put it to use.

How often have you been unable to think of somebody's name and said, "It will come to me later." And, sure enough, later when you are probably thinking about nothing in particular, out pops the name. Your subconscious computer has found it for you. There are a great many uses to which you can put your subconscious computer, not least of which is solving seemingly insuperable problems. But the use to which *you* want to put it is that of helping you to win or at least be successful in sports competitions.

14.9 The Power of Mental Rehearsal

When I did gymnastics I soon discovered that during, say, a rings routine the way in which I performed a particular move determined the choice of subsequent moves. If I wished to follow move 'a' with move 'b' I had to do move 'a' in a particular way lest I find upon completion of 'a', that move 'b' was not one of the available options. I would be obliged to perform move 'k' or 'p' instead. In other words I had to be thinking at least one move ahead. Tackling a complex routine in this way was a recipe for disaster, as the moves followed so fast on one another that sooner or later I was bound to make a mistake. The conscious mind could not think fast enough and eventually it would be overtaken by events.

The solution was to rehearse the routine in my head before its execution. I found the best place to do this was standing directly underneath the rings before mounting the apparatus. In this way I was able to picture the surroundings, as they would appear during the routine. However, I used to practise the routine, mentally, on all sorts of occasions in all sorts of places. The result was that my subconscious was able to take over the general execution of the routine freeing my conscious mind to concentrate on the finer points and pay special attention to the most difficult moves. My floor routine has been so firmly implanted in my subconscious in this way that even now, decades since I last performed it, I can still remember and visualise it. In fact I can visualise my horizontal bar routine and my rings routine exceptionally well. Also, 15 years after I had last vaulted, I found that my vault was still intact too. These were my best and favourite pieces of apparatus. The parallel bars were my next to worst piece and I am having difficulty remembering that routine, whilst I can barely recall any of my side horse routine, my least favourite piece. This must say something. The routines which I rehearsed mentally the most often were my best and the images of them are the most easily recalled.

Whilst I was writing this chapter the national rowing championships took place. Two girls from my club were entered in lightweight double sculls. After the event, in discussion, one of them described to me how whilst lying in the bath that morning she had sculled over the whole course in her head. This mental rehearsal had taken her exactly the same time as the race would be expected to take, even though she had her eyes closed and was therefore only aware of how long the rehearsal had taken when it was over and she had noticed the time on her watch. How did they get on in the race? They won the gold medal!

Mental rehearsal is used successfully by many sports people in a variety of sports. An eventer I once supported at a competition, having walked the cross-country course, subsequently jumped every fence mentally whilst warming up her horse. Every fence, that is, except one which was so easy she overlooked a mental rehearsal for it. You have probably guessed that the one fence she did not mentally rehearse was the only one where she and her horse had a problem. A costly oversight!

Weightlifters utilise enormous concentration in order to succeed in a lift. The level of concentration required is so intense that it may inhibit epileptic fits in those susceptible to them. I saw a TV programme about this once. Weightlifters have a problem though in that they have a time limit in which to perform their lift during a competition and it takes time to build up the level of concentration required for success. So for the supreme effort much mental rehearsal has to be done well before the event and psychological conditioning also, as described later in 14.11.

You may remember how I described in chapter 2 the benefit that teaching someone else brings to your own technique. This is a further example of the power of your subconscious mind.

14.10 Obtaining Access to Your Subconscious Computer at Will

Levels of consciousness vary. As I outlined in the first chapter you could score them out of 10.

10. The fire alarm had just gone off and it turns out to be a real fire. Frantic panic!

9. Alert and wide awake. The starter's gun has just gone off.

8. Alert, focused and in control. The starter's gun is about to go off.

7. Wide awake, busy.
6. Awake but not especially alert.
5. Normal.
4. Relaxed and unstressed.
3. Half asleep being only vaguely aware of what is going on around you.
2. Light sleep.
1. Deep sleep.
0. In a coma from which it is impossible to awaken.

You have to get yourself to level 3, the half asleep stage, in order to reach your subconscious.

At first you will find it easiest to do this in a quiet, darkened room though with experience you will find that you can do it anywhere. Ideally you should be sitting in a comfortable position (not lying) and able to relax your muscles. Finally close your eyes.

If you have difficulty relaxing your muscles visualise the various parts of your body starting with the tips of your toes. Let each part relax in turn. Don't make it relax, let it relax. If you are still having difficulty then try to tense each part before letting it relax so that you are sure of the difference. Work up your body a section at a time and by the time you have reached the top of your head you will be relaxed.

This physical relaxation will get you half way to the required level of mental relaxation. You can get yourself the rest of the way simply by counting yourself down from 1 to 20. You may have noticed a distinct similarity between these techniques and those used to induce a hypnotic state. This is hardly surprising and what you do in the way of mental rehearsal when you are at this low level of consciousness is essentially the same as the hypnotist does when implanting a suggestion in a subject's mind that will later be acted upon. The difference is that you are implanting the suggestion yourself. The power of the subconscious mind to arrange things so that the auto-suggestion is acted upon is so great that you must be very careful in the way you suggest things to yourself. You must not ask for the impossible to be achieved or the subsequent power of the subconscious computer will be impaired because of failure. You must not implant doubt or negative thoughts. Your goals must be realistic and achievable and when performing your mental rehearsal you must be very positive in your approach.

For example it would not be desirable to say to yourself "I will not lose my cool," because of the negative in the statement. The subconscious may only latch onto the words "lose my cool," or worse still "lose". Far better to say to yourself, "I always remain calm and collected." Note also how this positive statement is put in the present tense and in such a way that the required objective is reinforced as though it already exists.

An objective such as that of being unperturbed by opponents' remarks can be phrased thus, "my concentration is unshakeable" or better still "my concentration is resolute" eliminating any hint of a negative.

Such objectives are important to achieve. A friend of mind was left dumb founded on the start because just before the starter said, "Go!" her opponent said, "I'll get you, you bitch." She was so shocked by this that she lost concentration completely and lost the race by a considerable distance. I'm not encouraging you to make such remarks but it is as well to be mentally prepared for gamesmanship of this nature and not to allow it to deflect you from your purpose.

14.11 Psychological Conditioning

Whilst you can gain access to your subconscious in the way I have described this method should be reserved for one objective at a time because it is so powerful.

You may have a number of tasks that you wish your subconscious computer to achieve for you though. To do this you short list these objectives, stated in the positive way illustrated above, and read them to yourself (preferably out loud) just before you go to sleep at night and again each day when you wake up. You will be surprised how effective this method can be. Remember to avoid, at all costs, saying to yourself negative things such as a "I do not want to be last anymore," or a "I do not want to be stuck at this level of competition anymore". This last sentence illustrates just how easy it is to fall into the habit of stating things in a negative way. You see I should have written - Remember always to say positive things to yourself such as "I am beating X in a race" or "I am regional champion because I have the talent and I train harder than everybody else does in the region". Have faith in yourself, in the power of your subconscious, in your coach, in this book, if you like, and only bite off as much as you can chew.

It is not often that a sportsman or woman comes from nowhere to become a world champion. Usually they make steady progress up the ladder of success, achieving one objective after another, with the steps from one to the next always appearing tangible, within reach, plausible, not too far fetched. A coach might spot the talent of a future world champion in a novice but the novice would not accept the supreme accolade as even a remote possibility. However success at a lowly level will lead to attempts at greater things. Perhaps merely to qualify to compete at a national championship. The next year competition at the championship could be assumed and success might considered to be a place in the final. A fourth place could lead to the objective in the following year being a medal of any colour and the chance of international competition. And so on.

14.12 Personality Profiles

A number of studies have been done into the Personality Profiles of sports people. An interesting one undertaken by W. P. Morgan is described by the term of "the iceberg profile" which refers merely to the shape of a curve on a chart. Morgan found that compared with college norms, runners, oarsmen and wrestlers had lower than normal levels of tension, depression, anger, psychic fatigue and confusion but a higher than normal level of psychic vigour.

14.13 Changing your Personality

"So what?" you may well ask. People with this personality profile may be attracted to participate in these sports in the first place or those without it may drop out because they are unsuited. On the other hand the personality of participants in the sports may change as a result of participation. In any event if you consider that a change in your personality is desirable in order to achieve the success that you desire you can achieve this change by the use of daily declarations. Remember though not to use declarations such as "I do not suffer from tension" but instead to say something like "I am relaxed and in control." Always accentuate positive statements and avoid negative ones. The subconscious is powerful and has to be trained correctly.

14.14 Coping with Failure

Achieving success, as opposed to winning, has a lot to do with setting realistic objectives. Entering the national championships as your first ever competition is not usually sensible. Entering a local event to see how you get on and without any real expectation of winning is realistic. Then if you win that will be a bonus. Once you are competing regularly you will be able to gauge the likelihood of a win and you will be able to judge better how much more effort you need to put into your training and preparation in order to win.

Always remember though that despite your best efforts a better competitor may still beat you. The only way to be sure of winning is to be a world champion and even these get beaten sometimes. Unless you are leagues ahead of the second best in the world you will find other people uncomfortably close to you and on those occasions if they get everything right and you don't, they may win and you may lose. As most of you reading this will not be world champions it is important for me to put winning and losing into perspective for you.

In sports where everybody competes together, en masse, such as a marathon run there is only one winner. The larger the field, the smaller is the chance that you will be that winner and the smaller the field, the greater is the chance that you will be that winner. So if winning is all you want then be sure only to enter small events.

Of course, it would be stupid of me to contend that winning small events brings greater satisfaction than participating in big events. If that were so there would not be tens of thousands of competitors in the London marathon. And of course although there is only one overall winner there are many individual class winners in such events and there are many, many more people who measure their success by their times or their positions or often just by their achievement in finishing.

In sports organised with a draw such as tennis or bowls, 50 percent of the competitors are knocked out in the first round and 50 percent of the remainder are knocked out in the second-round and so on. So in the end there are many more apparent losers than winners. Many of these losers will be able to rationalise their loss by saying such things as; "Well I lost to the eventual winner." Very few people will come away from competition, totally dejected, and I submit that those who do are those who performed below their own personal expectations.

As Pierre de Coubertin said in 1908 "... the important thing in life is not victory but the struggle; the essential thing is not to have won but to have fought well....". As I mentioned earlier this is often misquoted as, "it is not the winning, but the taking part that is important" and in the misquotation an essential truth is lost, for in participation alone one gains little satisfaction. It is in the fighting well that the satisfaction is gained. To come away from a competition knowing that you gave your all and you produced your best performance is to come away well pleased and satisfied.

It is for this reason that a competition that is won easily is of little satisfaction to the winner who does not have to give his or her best performance. This is why people of international standard go to international competitions, seeking out sports people of a similar standard and with whom they can have a good "struggle" or "fight". The best and most memorable competitions for competitors and spectators alike are those that are most closely fought and where the lead changes constantly so the result is unpredictable. The satisfaction gained by winning such a close competition is far greater than that of winning easily and the loser gains almost as much satisfaction. Indeed the loser who had no expectations and never thought to be in with a chance may gain even greater satisfaction than the winner.

In your competitive life if you wish to gain satisfaction from your sport then you will have to seek out close competition. This means leaving behind those who are of a low standard whom you can beat easily and finding your own level. Unless you are of world champion standard you will lose at least as often as you win and it is important to have this perspective if you are going to cope with the failure of not winning. The only times you should be disappointed are those when you fail to meet your own standards. Surprising as it may seem, it frequently occurs that a winner is disappointed in this way, having performed badly but won nevertheless.

14.15 Dealing with Disappointment

Sometimes circumstances arise or accidents happen that prevent you succeeding, when all other things being equal, you would have achieved your objective. The disappointment, not to say anguish, felt on such occasions can lead to great sorrow and even cause you to give up the sport that until then was your greatest love in life. This is quite different from the disappointment arising out of a failure to meet up to your own expectations. The word, tragedy, is often used in describing such events.

We have all witnessed them, even if we have not all been directly involved in them. A famous example is the time that Mary Decker-Slaney tripped on Zola Bud in the Los Angeles Olympics. She was thus robbed of the Olympic gold medal that had already eluded her once at Moscow because of the American boycott of the 1980 games.

Usually such bitter disappointment, the type that leads to buckets of tears, particularly among women but not exclusively so, follows a long build-up of preparation and expectation. A high goal has been set and great deal of hard work undertaken. Success seems within your reach and then just as your moment of glory approaches it is snatched from you buy fate. Time heals the wounds of disappointment but scars often remain.

I coached two girls in a double scull with the objective of winning a medal of the national rowing championships. They knew they were capable of the required standard because they had already, comfortably beaten the previous year's bronze medallists. So they trained hard, twice a day most days. They were the most dedicated athletes that it had been my privilege to coach up until then. Unfortunately, the only competition over the same 2000m distance in their boat class that they could enter before the championships, was an international regatta. But that race experience was vital to them in their preparation. So we entered fully expecting to come last. Our expectations were fulfilled but an awful lot was learned and they were encouraged by not being outclassed. The only other competition that they were able to find in this boat class was a local one over 1,000m, which they won easily, crushing their opposition in the first few strokes.

On the big day though, they were lying in the third place with only 250m to go when they struck a lane marker buoy, which stopped them in their tracks. They set off again only to hit another buoy and to breakdown in tears. The three crews that beat them got the three medals and they were left empty handed. All that training and nothing to show for it except a trophy from the local regatta that meant little to them. For one of the girls her enjoyment of the sport faded away and she left it to take up triathlon. The other carried on but has not reached the same heights since. I myself became disillusioned for a long while. I felt very responsible having demanded such dedication from them for such little reward. It was this lack of reward that was my fault. I had not given them sufficient opportunity to race, even if at the wrong distance, because I was obsessed with tuning them optimally for the endurance event that 2000m actually is. If they had won a few other trophies along the way, or at least had some worthwhile and memorable races, the disappointment would not have been so great.

So the major method of dealing with disappointment is prevention rather than cure. The more often you expose yourself to competition the more opportunities you give yourself for obtaining a reward for all your efforts. Of course, it has to be said that victory over vastly inferior opponents is not all that gratifying. Remember also that at the very highest level at which you are capable of competing, you will have to call upon every physical and mental resource available to you and you can only do this a few times a year. However, if you are a wise and experienced competitor you can make these superhuman efforts on the important occasions whilst still competing regularly in the sport you so love. The trick is not to expect to win when it does not really matter and to be prepared to treat competition as part of your training. This means a) not necessarily being properly prepared for and b) not deliberately tuning for a competition that does not really matter. If you win, so much the better.

That said, any international athlete would tell you that the winner of an event at an international meeting is not likely to be remembered, but the winner of the Olympic gold medal will be remembered. It is for this reason that you should not leave anything to chance. You should have everything planned down to the finest detail and contingency plans for the things that might go wrong. Because the chance you get at the BIG ONE, may be your only chance.

14.16 Routines

Routines can play a good part in the preparation for an event. A routine for packing your kit bag so that you do not forget your spare shoe laces. A routine for eating before and during an event. A routine for the training during the week running up to a competition. A routine for warming up. Routines have their place but you should be careful not to become superstitious about them. If you come to rely on your routines too much then when something happens to break the routine your psychological preparedness can be impaired. Routines are fine but do not let a break in your routine upset you.

Be pragmatic and practical. Try to turn negatives into positives. Always look on the bright side. If, when you get into the office somebody says to you, "Miserable day, isn't it?" be sure to reply, "It's nice and warm in here though, isn't it?"

If, for example, a family crisis or very long journey or a couple of days of hay fever has upset your normal race week program, do not let it get on top of you. Examine your situation and adapt to it positively. It may turn out that the enforced rest has been opportune and you perform better than ever.

Imagine this. You are about to compete in the Olympic final. You get up full of expectation and go to get your breakfast. There is nobody around. You go to get the bus to your venue. There are no buses. What is going through your head? How are you going to get there? You have trained for years for this. What is going on? You pinch yourself, convinced that you must just be having a nightmare. But no this is really happening. In fact this really did happen the morning after the bombing at Atlanta in 1996. Many athletes found themselves in this situation. At a coaching conference, Miles Forbes-Thomas the coach of the British single sculler, Peter Haining, described eloquently how the mature and well-prepared team of athlete, coach and manager handled the situation. They had already hired a car for just this sort of contingency and they set about implementing "Plan B" without fretting about matters that were outside of their control.

This is the secret, control the controllables and don't cry over spilt milk. There is absolutely no point in fretting over something over which you have no control.

14.17 Turning Weakness into Strength

In training you may never find your weaknesses but in competition your opponents most surely will. When they do you may suffer a defeat. This is not cause for dismay, however. You will have learned a valuable lesson and now you can capitalise on this newfound knowledge so that your weakness becomes strength. The next person who tries to capitalise on your flaw will come unstuck and may in turn be defeated.

Those parts of our sports that we least enjoy tend to be the parts at which we are least successful. By practising hard at those parts we enjoy least, we can become good at them. Then we become successful at them. Then, surprise, surprise we find that we enjoyed our success and then we enjoy things we used to loathe.

Work on your weaknesses. Be positive about them. Do not let them get on top of you lest you be beaten before you start.

14.18 Enjoy Your Sport

A final philosophical point rather than psychological. You must enjoy your training as well as your competition. This is why we do sport. Because we enjoy it. The day that you realise that you are no longer enjoying your sport is the day you should give it up and seek another one. I do not recommend that you give up sport altogether. The challenge of mastering a new skill is a most rewarding one, often more enjoyable than competing at a high level. Just think back to your novice days and remember the buzz you used to get then. If you have stopped enjoying your sport for the time being, maybe it is time to put back into it some of what you have already got out by teaching youngsters what you already know. Their enthusiasm is infectious and you can be an inspiration to them. Try it. You may be able to achieve more with them than you ever could yourself.

But above all, enjoy it. Enjoy every fleeting moment of it. Go back to the goals that you set at the beginning of this book and make sure that enjoyment of your sport is one of them. Acknowledge that the journey is sometimes more important than the destination. This is a lesson for life.

Try to step back from your situation and observe it as an outsider. Realise how lucky you are. Savour every moment and lock it in your memory.

15 TAKE AWAYS

What are the two overriding messages in this book? Well I think the first one has to be specificity, specificity, specificity, specificity, specificity, specificity and specificity. You can waste a lot of time and effort training the wrong things, to no avail. You can blunder on with bad technique, practising and grooving faults and you will get nowhere fast. Not only does PERFECT PRACTICE MAKE PERFECT but it also trains the correct muscles! The effect of training is so specific that the training of muscles other than those required for your specific sport's action is largely a waste of time except insofar as it may prevent injury.

And when I say, "trains the right muscles" I do not just mean for the acquisition of strength or speed. That is only one benefit. Many improvements required for endurance also take place in muscles. And not just in the muscles of the heart and the breathing muscles. Considerable beneficial physiological changes take place in the motor muscles, the ones you use to make the actions required by your sport. So learn your skills well and learn what is required in your sport to achieve good performance then practise in ways that are specific in as many aspects as possible. Specific in speed, specific in range of movement, specific in load, specific in energy system use, specific in as many ways as you can think.

And the second message is that anything is possible if you want it enough. The most successful sports people are often quoted as having "dreamt of this moment from an early age". They have envisaged themselves achieving their goal time and again. They probably have pictures of their sporting heroes on their bedroom walls and they visualise emulating their achievements, possibly without realising just what a powerful effect this has on their subconscious. So if you clearly set out your goals, do your daily declarations and visualise your success then your subconscious will work out for you how to achieve your objectives for you. The importance of this cannot be underestimated. You can use the techniques I have outlined to achieve almost anything in life that you want, not just success in sport.

That is it really. The success you want to achieve is there for the taking. I have given you all the necessary tools to go out there and do it. Be sure to turn every negative into a positive. As Oscar Wilde said,

"We are all of us lying in the gutter. But some of us are looking at the stars."

And if you reach for the stars you may at least get to heaven! It may take a while but you can get there. You may need to learn from other sources but at least now you know what you are looking for. I guarantee that if you follow the guidelines I have laid out in this book then you will be successful. Go do it!

ABOUT THE AUTHOR

Stephen Walker holds the highest qualification in coaching rowing that it is possible to attain in Britain. He is also a qualified physical education teacher. But these qualifications were really obtained so that he could improve his own performances because, when he graduated as an engineer, it was not possible to study sports science. The university courses simply didn't exist.

But Steve was hungry for any information that would enable him to perform better and so he devoured course material and text books recommended by all those he encountered.

Yet, inevitably, all through his rowing career he has been disseminating this useful knowledge to others and has developed a deep understanding of what it takes to win. Steve says that his specialist skill is in realising the potential of others. "Most people have no idea what their potential is, even talented people, and certainly not newcomers to a sport. But with my guidance they eventually achieve far more than they ever dreamt they could achieve because actually, they never really dreamt at all! They just had no idea what their potential was."

Steve has been head coach at Oxford Polytechnic, now Oxford Brookes University, Liverpool University and Manchester University and when he was in each of these posts the clubs attained much higher achievements than they ever had previously.

Still today at the age of 62 Steve is competing (and winning) as a master at local, regional, national and international events. He is driven to challenge himself and to challenge others.

Made in the USA
San Bernardino, CA
31 March 2020